ACADEMIC WORD POWER 3

ACADEMIC WORD POWER 3

Pat Bull

Series Editor: Donna Obenda
University of North Texas

HEINLE
CENGAGE Learning·

Australia • Brazil • Japan • Korea • Mexico • Singapore • Spain • United Kingdom • United States

HEINLE
CENGAGE Learning·

Academic Word Power 3
Pat Bull
Series Editor: Donna Obenda

Editor in Chief: Patricia A. Coryell

Director of ESL Publishing: Susan Maguire

Senior Development Editor: Kathleen
 Sands-Boehmer

Editorial Assistant: Evangeline Bermas

Cover Design manager: Diana Coe

Marketing Manager: Annamarie Rice

ISBN-13: 978-0-618-39770-9

ISBN-10: 0-618-39770-1

Heinle
20 Channel Center Street
Boston, MA 02210
USA

Cengage Learning is a leading provider of customized learning solutions with
office locations around the globe, including Singapore, the United Kingdom,
Australia, Mexico, Brazil, and Japan. Locate your local office at
www.cengage.com/global

Cengage Learning products are represented in Canada by Nelson Education, Ltd.

Visit Heinle online at **elt.heinle.com**

Visit our corporate website at **www.cengage.com**

Printed in the United States of America
8 9 10 11 12   20 19 18 17 16

CONTENTS

UNIT 5

WORDS

aggregate	explicit	publication	topic
comprise	incentive	release	transmission
contradiction	initiative	reverse	ultimately
domain	interval	subsidiary	visible
edition	prohibit	survive	voluntary

UNIT 6

WORDS

adaptation	differentiation	hierarchical	revision
allocation	disposal	incidence	scope
clarity	empirical	incorporate	submit
convert	extract	inhibition	termination
definite	finite	prospect	trace

INTRODUCTION

WELCOME TO *ACADEMIC WORD POWER*!

ACADEMIC WORD POWER is a four-volume vocabulary series for students of English at the high school or college level who are planning to pursue further academic studies. The goal of the series is to help students learn the vocabulary they need for success in academic reading and writing.

ACADEMIC WORD POWER 1 is designed for intermediate students.

ACADEMIC WORD POWER 2, 3, and *4* are designed for high-intermediate, advanced, and high-advanced levels, respectively.

The target vocabulary in all four volumes was selected from the Academic Word List (AWL) developed by Averil Coxhead in 1998. The AWL, which contains 570 words, was compiled from a corpus of 3.5 million words found in academic texts. When students add the words from this list to a basic vocabulary of 2000 words, they will be able to comprehend approximately 90 percent of the vocabulary in academic texts. When proper nouns and technical vocabulary are added to this, students approach the 95 percent comprehension level that research has shown is needed for successful academic reading.

TO THE TEACHER . . .

Series Approach

Reflecting the latest research in vocabulary acquisition and pedagogy, the exercises and activities in this text are based on an interactive approach to vocabulary instruction. Consequently, the reading, writing and speaking exercises give the student multiple exposures to the target words in meaningful contexts and provide rich information about each word. The exercises also establish ties between the target words and the student's prior knowledge and experience.

About the Books

Each volume has seven units that target 20 AWL words per unit. Thus, 140 AWL words are studied in each book, and 560 of the 570 words on the AWL are covered in the four volumes. The AWL words were sequenced and grouped into the four volumes by taking into consideration the frequency of the words, their level of difficulty and the thematic relationships between the words. A great variety of vocabulary development practice activities as well as strategies for learning and remembering academic vocabulary are incorporated in each book.

Text Organization

The seven units in each book are divided into four lessons that focus on five AWL words. Every lesson includes the following components:

- **Word Families:** This section introduces the five target words by providing a head word, which is the most frequently used in academic texts, as well as other word forms of the target word. A chart is provided for students to place the different word forms under the correct part of speech. This focus on word families helps students decipher new words and build spelling proficiency.

- **Reading:** A one-paragraph reading introduces students to the five target words in an academic context.

- **Comprehension Check:** Two exercises check students' superficial comprehension of the target words. For the first exercise, students match definitions by using the context provided in the reading in the previous section. The second exercise includes exercises such as true/false statements, yes/no questions, odd man out, fill in the blank, or matching sentence halves.

- **Word Study:** This section provides rich instruction through exercises that offer an expansion of the target words. This is accomplished through a wide variety of exercises, such as collocations, multiple meanings, grammar application, word form practice, analogies, pronunciation tips, and idiomatic usage. Both the written exercises in this section and the previous section are designed to be completed quickly by students and graded easily by teachers because research shows that the type of written exercise is not significant in terms of retention. Rather, it is the number of retrievals that is significant. Thus, it is better to have a larger quantity of exercises that can be done quickly as opposed to a smaller number of exercises that are time-consuming to complete (such as writing original sentences with the target words).

Using Words in Communication: Communicative activities in this section give students practice in using the target words fluently. The students use the target words orally in different settings, such as sentence completion, discussion, role-play, interviewing, summariz ing, paraphrasing, storytelling, listing ideas related to the target word, or associating the target word with other words from the unit. These activities aid in retention of the target words as they develop a link between the target words and students' past experience and knowledge.

Other features of the series include:

- **Unit Reviews:** Each unit ends with an exercise that reviews all 20 words from the unit through an easy-to-do, fun activity, such as a crossword puzzle, find-a-word, word scramble, sentence scramble, associations, and definition match-up.

- **Website:** All four volumes have a companion website with an instructor and student site. This site can be accessed at elt.thomson.com/wordpower. the instructor site includes unit assessments and the answer key for the book. The student site includes longer readings with the target AWL words, vocabulary flashcards, and review quizzes for each lesson.

- **Easy to supplement with writing activities:** If a teacher wants to do more extensive writing practice with the target words, the books can be easily supplemented with writing activities such as writing original sentences, paragraphs and essays with the AWL words.

TO THE STUDENT . . .

Did you know the following facts?

- The average native English-speaking university student has a vocabulary of around 21,000 words.

- The average adult ESL student learns about 2,500 English words per year.

Before you get depressed and discouraged, consider the following fact: English (like any other language) uses a relatively small number of words over and over again. Words that are used over and over again are called "high frequency" words. The words you will be studying in this book come from a high frequency list called the *Academic Word List* (AWL). The AWL contains 570 words that frequently occur in academic texts, such as university textbooks, course workbooks, and academic journal articles.

Why is it a good use of your time and energy to learn the words on the AWL?

If you add the 570 words on the AWL list to a basic vocabulary of 2000 English words (which most intermediate readers already have), you'll be able to understand 90% of the words in an average academic text. This book will help you learn many of the words on the AWL through numerous written exercises that introduce you to the meanings of the words and provide important information about the words, such as word forms, idiomatic uses, and pronunciation tips. This book also has many speaking activities that will give you practice using the new words fluently.

Besides completing all the exercises in the book, it is recommended that you use vocabulary cards to help you remember the new words. On the next page are some tips (advice) on how to make vocabulary cards.

HOW TO MAKE YOUR OWN VOCABULARY CARDS

1. Use small cards (no bigger than 3 by 5 inch) so that they can be easily carried.

2. Put the new word on one side and the definition (meaning) on the other side.

3. In addition to the definition, you can include the following information on the back side of the card:

   • a translation of the new word in your language;
   • pictures or diagrams related to the new word;
   • phonetic pronunciation;
   • a sample sentence using the new word.

4. Practice with the cards by looking at the new word and trying to recall the meaning first, and then (later) by looking at the meaning and trying to recall the new word.

5. Say the words aloud or to yourself when you are studying the cards.

6. Study the cards frequently. When you learn a new word, try to study it later that day, the next day, the next week, and then a few weeks later.

7. Study the words with a partner occasionally. When reviewing with a partner, try to use the word in a new sentence.

8. Change the order of the cards frequently. Don't order the cards alphabetically or put the cards in groups of similar words. Words which look the same or have similar meanings are easy to confuse.

GUIDE TO PRONUNCIATION

Vowels

Symbol	Key Word	Pronunciation
/ɑ/	hot	/hɑt/
/æ/	cat	/kæt/
/aɪ/	tie	/taɪ/
/aʊ/	cow	/kaʊ/
/ɛ/	bed	/bɛd/
/eɪ/	same	/seɪm/
/i/	he	/hɪ/
/ɪ/	it	/ɪt/
/oʊ/	go	/goʊ/
/ʊ/	book	/bʊk/
/ɔ/	dog	/dɔg/
/ɔɪ/	boy	/bɔɪ/
/ʌ/	cup	/kʌp/
/ɜr/	bird	/bɜrd/
/ə/	about	/əˈbaʊt/
	softer	/ˈsɔftər/

Consonants

Symbol	Key Word	Pronunciation
/b/	be	/bi/
/d/	did	/dɪd/
/dʒ/	jump	/dʒʌmp/
/f/	fat	/fæt/
/g/	go	/goʊ/
/h/	hit	/hɪt/
/k/	cat	/kæt/
/l/	life	/laɪf/
/m/	me	/mi/
/n/	no	/noʊ/
/ŋ/	sing	/sɪŋ/
/p/	pen	/pɛn/
/r/	red	/rɛd/
/s/	see	/si/
/t/	tea	/ti/
/tʃ/	cheap	/tʃip/
/v/	vote	/voʊt/
/w/	we	/wi/
/z/	zoo	/zʊ/
/ð/	they	/ðeɪ/
/θ/	thin	/θɪn/

GUIDE TO SYLLABLE STRESS

/ˈ/   open   /ˈoʊpən/
used before a syllable to show primary stress

/ˌ/   doorway   /ˈdɔrˌweɪ/
used before a syllable to show secondary stress

ACKNOWLEDGEMENTS

Many thanks to Averil Coxhead for giving us permission to use the *Academic Word List* (AWL) in the development of this series. It is hard to imagine the hours of planning and labor that went into compiling this list from such an extensive corpus (3.5 million running words from over 400 academic texts). For more information about the AWL see the article *A New Academic Word List* by Averil Coxhead in the Summer 2000 TESOL Quarterly.

Also, thanks to Barbara Hefka, an instructor at the University of North Texas Intensive English Language Institute (IELI) for sequencing and grouping the 570 words on the AWL for the four volumes in this series. When sequencing these words, Barbara had to take in consideration the frequency of the words, their level of difficulty, and thematic relationships between the words. It was a herculean task that only someone with Barbara's breadth of ESL experience and teaching intuition could have handled so well.

Huge thanks go to Judith Kulp, a publishing coordinator at UNT, for her invaluable, professional input on this project. Thanks also go to M. J. Weaver for her production skills, and to Yun Ju Kim, a communication design student at UNT, who created the graphics for the series.

Finally, thanks to Eva Bowman, Director of the IELI, and Dr. Rebecca Smith-Murdock, Director of International Programs, for their support in the development of the series. They had faith in my vision for the series and in the writing and creative abilities of the four authors: Lisa Hollinger, Celia Thompson, Pat Bull, and Barbara Jones.

- Donna Obenda

My special thanks to:

Donna Obenda, who had the vision for a series of vocabulary books based on the AWL, and had the confidence in me as one of the authors. Donna was an encourager and advisor through every stage and page of this project.

My fellow IELI instructors who taught this book and made it better. The final project is a group effort and not the work of one person.

My family members who helped me through the writing stage — Matthew, Kathryn, Dennis, Ivan and Dorris Bull.

- Pat Bull

UNIT 1

WORDS

amendment	derive	migration	recovery
assume	enforcement	motivation	revealed
attribute	exposure	nevertheless	transport
conflict	generate	parameter	underlying
constraint	isolate	ratio	utility

READINGS
Who Did it?
Learn English Through Latin
How to Change the Constitution
The Balance of Science and Nature

STRATEGIES AND SKILLS
Word Forms
- Word family chart
- Word form selection

Comprehension Check
- Matching definitions
- Identifying synonyms

Word Expansion
- Grammar application
- Collocations
- Multiple meaning
- Idiomatic usage
- Usage in specific domains

Interactive Speaking Practice
- Sentence completion
- Listing

ACADEMIC WORD POWER

LESSON 1

A. WORD FAMILIES
Study the five word families below. Then fill in the word form chart. The underlined word forms at the top of the list are the most commonly used forms in academic texts.

conflict (2X)*	enforcement	exposure	motivation	underlying
/ˈkɑnflɪkt/	/ɛnˈfɔrsmənt/	/ɪkˈspouʒər/	/moutəˈveʃən/	/ˈʌndərˌlaɪɪŋ/
conflicting	enforce	expose	motive	underlie
		exposed	motivate	
			motivated	
			motivating	
			unmotivated	

* used 2 times in the word form chart

Exercise - Word Form Chart

NOUN	VERB	ADJECTIVE	ADVERB
1. conflict	1.	1.	
1. enforcement	1.		
1. exposure	1.	1.	
1. motivation 2.	1.	1. 2. 3.	
	1.	1. underlying	

B. READING

Who Did It?

When law <u>enforcement</u> officers investigate a murder, they search for any <u>underlying</u> causes of <u>conflict</u>, such as a marital conflict or a dispute over money. Sometimes finding the <u>motivation</u> for a crime leads to the <u>exposure</u> of the criminal.

C. COMPREHENSION CHECK
Exercise 1
Refer to the reading above and use the context to guess the meanings of the words below. Then match the words to their definitions. Do NOT use a dictionary.

   ___ 1. conflict   A. a position of being unprotected, uncovered

   ___ 2. enforcement   B. supporting, located beneath

   ___ 3. exposure   C. a disagreement, an argument, or a war

   ___ 4. motivation   D. the reason to do something

   ___ 5. underlying   E. the act of making people obey laws and rules

Exercise 2
Which word does not belong?

1. conflict	argument	disunity	factor
2. enforcement	desire	rules	force
3. exposure	uncovering	negative	unmasking
4. underlying	exterior	beneath	supporting
5. motivation	encouragement	unhappiness	impetus

D. WORD STUDY
Exercise 1
Many words in English are commonly used with certain prepositions. Find the following words in the reading, and write the prepositions that go with them on the line provided.
(Hint: In our reading, one of these words is not used with a preposition, but it often is. Can you guess which preposition would fit?)

   1. exposure   _____

   2. motivation   _____

   3. enforcement   _____

Other words in English are commonly used with certain nouns. Find the following vocabulary word in the reading, and write the noun that goes with it on the line provided.

   4. underlying   _____

Exercise 2

Conflict of interest is a special expression in English. It is used when one activity conflicts with another activity so that the ability of a person to act honestly is questioned. Read the following examples of **conflict of interest**.

Write YES if the expression is used correctly or NO if it is not.

_____ 1. There could be a <u>conflict of interest</u> if a judge had to decide the guilt or innocence of his own son.

_____ 2. The student had a <u>conflict of interest</u> in deciding between a major in physics or chemistry. She excelled in both.

_____ 3. If a government official owned stock in Lockheed Corporation and then gave a government contract to Lockheed to build new military fighter jets it would be a <u>conflict of interest</u>.

E. USING WORDS IN COMMUNICATION
Exercise

With a partner, read and complete the following sentences.

1. An example of a <u>conflict</u> I have been involved in is…

2. My <u>motivation</u> for studying hard is...

3. The <u>enforcement</u> of laws is done primarily by…

4. Newspapers often <u>expose</u> political wrongdoing. One scandal that has gotten a lot of media <u>exposure</u> is…

5. One <u>underlying</u> cause of some students' poor performance on tests is…

LESSON 2

A. WORD FAMILIES

Study the five word families below. Then fill in the word form chart. The underlined word forms at the top of the list are the most commonly used forms in academic texts.

assume	attribute (2X)	derive	nevertheless	reveal
/əˈsum/	/əˈtrɪbut/	/dɪrˈaɪv/	/ˌnɛvərðəˈlɛs/	/rəˈvil/
assumption	attribution	derivation		revealing
	attributable	derivative		revelation

Exercise - Word Form Chart

NOUN	VERB	ADJECTIVE	ADVERB
1.	1. assume		
1. 2.	1. attribute	1.	
1. 2.	1. derive		
			1. nevertheless
1.	1. reveal	1.	

B. READING

Learn English Through Latin

Many English words are <u>derived</u> from Latin, so if students learn the meanings of common Latin roots, prefixes, and suffixes, the meanings of many English words are <u>revealed</u>. A good vocabulary in American university students is often <u>attributed</u> to some background knowledge of Latin. <u>Nevertheless</u>, one cannot <u>assume</u> that **not** knowing Latin would cause a student to have a poor vocabulary.

C. COMPREHENSION CHECK
Exercise 1
Refer to the reading above and use the context to guess the meanings of the words below. Then match the words to their definitions. Do NOT use a dictionary.

_____ 1. assume   A. uncovered something secret
_____ 2. attributed   B. in spite of that, however
_____ 3. derived   C. gave credit to, explained the reason for
_____ 4. nevertheless   D. came from
_____ 5. revealed   E. to believe something is true without knowing

Exercise 2
Yes or No? Answer the question with YES if the vocabulary word is used correctly and NO if it is not.

_____ 1. Please don't <u>assume</u> the chemical compound.

_____ 2. Skin cancer is often <u>attributed</u> to too much sun exposure.

_____ 3. Olive oil is <u>derived</u> from olives.

_____ 4. He enjoys his class. <u>Nevertheless</u>, he goes to class regularly.

_____ 5. The congressman had to resign when his secret was <u>revealed</u>.

D. Word Study
Exercise 1
Choose the correct word form for each blank. You may need to change verb and nouns endings.

1. The _____ that the earth was flat was believed before Columbus discovered America.
   a. assume   b. assumption   c. assuming

2. Psychiatrists _____ the mental disorder schizophrenia to a brain chemistry problem.
   a. attribute   b. attribution   c. attributable

3. The English word credible is a _____ of the Latin word credibilis.
   a. derive   b. derivative   c. derived

4. The Italian farmer who, while digging on his land, accidentally discovered the wall of ancient Pompeii, was shocked by the _____ .
   a. revealed   b. revelation   c. revealing

Exercise 2
Many words have more than one meaning. Consider the following meanings of the word
assume.

> 1. assume (v) - to think something is true without knowing or having proof
>
> 2. assume (v) - to take on responsibility for

Choose which meaning for **assume** is used in each of the following sentences.

___ 1. Many college students <u>assume</u> their parents will pay their bills, so they are not careful with their spending.

___ 2. Law professors <u>assume</u> their students have read the assigned case studies before attending lectures each week.

___ 3. After a US presidential election in November, the newly elected president <u>assumes</u> power the following January.

___ 4. The famous Italian mathematician Fibonacci <u>assumed</u> the rabbits in his experiments were physically mature enough to mate at 2 months of age.

___ 5. The purchaser can <u>assume</u> the previous loan on the home with its 5.6% interest rate.

E. USING WORDS IN COMMUNICATION
Exercise - Lists

1. List three things people <u>assume</u> about you.

2. List three things that are <u>derived</u> from rice.

3. When you perform well on tests, what three things can you <u>attribute</u> your success to?

4. List three things life to this point has <u>revealed</u> to you about yourself.

5. List three things you don't know how to do well but, <u>nevertheless</u>, choose to do.

LESSON 3

A. WORD FAMILIES

Study the five word families below. Then fill in the word form chart. The underlined word forms at the top of the list are the most commonly used forms in academic texts.

amendment	constraint	isolate	parameter	ratio
/ə'mɛndmənt/	/kɑn'steɪnt/	/'aisəleitəd/	/pə'ræmetər/	/'reɪʃou/
amend	constrain	isolated		
amended	constrained	isolation		
	constraining	isolationism		
	unconstrained			

Exercise - Word Form Chart

NOUN	VERB	ADJECTIVE	ADVERB
1. amendment	1.	1.	
1. constraint	1.	1. 2. 3.	
1. 2.	1. isolate	1.	
1. parameter			
1. ratio			

B. READING

How to Change the Constitution

The Constitution of the United States can only be changed by passing an <u>amendment</u>. There are strict <u>parameters</u> on how this is done. In both houses of Congress, there must be a <u>ratio</u> of 2 to 3 in favor of an issue before an amendment can be proposed. These <u>constraints</u> prevent one <u>isolated</u> group of citizens from having its cause accepted as a constitutional right. Once an amendment has been established, the guidelines for removing it are just as strict.

C. COMPREHENSION CHECK
Exercise 1
Refer to the reading above and use the context to guess the meanings of the words below. Then match the words to their definitions. Do NOT use a dictionary.

___ 1. amendment	A. a relationship between two numbers
___ 2. constraints	B. a change or modification
___ 3. isolated	C. standards that define an activity
___ 4. parameters	D. limitations
___ 5. ratio	E. separated from others, alone

Exercise 2
Which word does not belong?

1.	amendment	revision	limitation	modification
2.	limits	rules	constraints	freedom
3.	alone	lonely	isolated	sick
4.	ratio	numbers	letters	rate
5.	standard	parameter	guideline	pleasure

D. WORD STUDY
Exercise 1
Many words in English are commonly used with certain prepositions. Look at the four words from this lesson below and the prepositions that commonly follow them.

amendment to	isolated from	ratio of	parameters for

Fill in the blanks below with the correct word and its common preposition.

1. When you live far from your family, you feel _____ them.

2. Our class has 10 males and 5 females, so the _____ males to females in our class is 2 to 1.

3. The teacher set the _____ our research project.

4. To propose an _____ the US Constitution requires a two thirds vote in both houses of Congress.

Exercise 2
To make amends is a special expression in English. **Amends** as a noun means an apology or gift to pay back for something wrong someone has done. **To make amends** is used to explain this action.

Write YES if **to make amends** is used correctly, or NO if it is not.

_____ 1. I forgot my mother's birthday, so I <u>made amends</u> by taking her to her favorite play and out to her favorite restaurant.

_____ 2. The engineer <u>made amends</u> to the computer design.

_____ 3. The teacher kept the students working in class 30 minutes late. She <u>made amends</u> the next day by ending class 30 minutes early.

E. USING WORDS IN COMMUNICATION
Exercise
Discuss these questions with your partner.

1. What <u>constraints</u> are you currently experiencing in your life?

2. Describe a time you felt <u>isolated</u> from those around you.

3. In your opinion, what is the ideal <u>ratio</u> of male to female students in a classroom situation. Why?

4. Describe a time you had to <u>make amends</u> after doing something wrong.

5. What were your parents' <u>parameters</u> for your behavior in adolescence?

LESSON 4

A. WORD FAMILIES

Study the five word families below. Then fill in the word form chart. The underlined word forms at the top of the list are the most commonly used forms in academic texts.

generate	migration	recovery	transport	utility
/ˈdʒɛnəˌreɪt/	/maɪˈɡreɪʃən/	/riˈkʌvəri/	/trænsˈpɔrt/	/ˈyutɪləti/
	migrant	recover	transporter	utilize
	migrating	recovering	transportation	utilization
	migratory	recoverable		
	migrate			

Exercise - Word Form Chart

NOUN	VERB	ADJECTIVE	ADVERB
	1. generate		
1. migration 2.	1.	1. 2.	
1. recovery	1.	1. 2.	
1. 2.	1. transport		
1. utility 2.	1.		

B. READING

The Balance of Science and Nature

The need for more power <u>generated</u> the idea for the Alaskan Pipeline. It <u>transports</u> oil across the state of Alaska to places that need it. Critics of the project were concerned about the slow <u>recovery</u> of the sensitive environment after the construction of the line. However, part of the <u>utility</u> of the line is that it is elevated high above the ground so that it does not prevent the <u>migration</u> of large elk herds. This is an example of science in balance with nature.

C. COMPREHENSION CHECK
Exercise 1
Refer to the reading above and use the context to guess the meanings of the words below.
Then match the words to their definitions. Do NOT use a dictionary.

_____ 1. generated   A. made happen, produced, created
_____ 2. migration   B. to move, to carry from one place to another
_____ 3. transport   C. the movement from one place to another
_____ 4. recovery   D. usefulness, a needed service
_____ 5. utility   E. regaining a loss

Exercise 2
Cross out the word that does not belong in each group.

1. migration	movement	immigrant	travel
2. transport	join	carry	convey
3. recover	rely	restore	regain
4. generate	produce	originate	recover
5. utility	usefulness	value	easy

D. WORD STUDY
Exercise 1
In the English language, certain words are used together regularly and sound correct together. These are called collocations. For example, a common collocation with <u>urban</u>, one of the words from this unit, is <u>urban migration</u>. Look at other collocations for the words from this unit. Try to guess the correct answers focusing on the meanings you've learned for the vocabulary words in this unit.

urban migration	transport company	recover from	generate support

Circle the letter of the correct answer for these collocations.

1. If a family became part of an <u>urban migration</u>, what would they do?
   a. both husband and wife work full time
   b. move from the countryside to the city in search of work
   c. live in an apartment rather than a house

2. A <u>transport company</u> would be in the business of
   a. financial services
   b. moving goods from one location to another
   c. energy, such as oil or electricity

3. If the economy is going to <u>recover from</u> a recession there needs to be
   a. an increase in unemployment
   b. a decrease in available products
   c. an increase in available jobs

4. Which of the following could <u>generate support</u> for increased taxes on air travel?
   a. the need for an increased number of government safety officers at airports
   b. a decline in jet fuel prices
   c. newer airplanes with smaller seats

Exercise 2

Recover is often used in connection with health. A **recovery room** is a special room in a hospital where patients are taken and observed after surgery.

Write YES if **recovery** or **recover** is used correctly or NO if it is not.

_____ 1. The nurse monitored the patient in the <u>recovery</u> room.

_____ 2. The student failed his exam, so he went to the <u>recovery</u> room.

_____ 3. The <u>recovery</u> time after surgery can vary from person to person.

_____ 4. Burn victims face a lengthy <u>recovery</u>.

_____ 5. Abdullah was taken to a special rehabilitation center to <u>recover</u> after his car accident.

_____ 6. The <u>recovery</u> of the hole in the road made driving much easier.

E. USING WORDS IN COMMUNICATION

Exercise

With a partner, read and complete the following.

1. The hardest thing I have had to <u>recover</u> from was…

2. The kinds of commercials that <u>generate</u> my interest are…

3. My favorite means of <u>transportation</u> is…

4. Many people in the United States <u>migrated</u> from…

REVIEW

The crossword puzzle below contains all 20 words from Unit 1.
Solve the puzzle by filling in the blanks to complete the sentences on the next page.

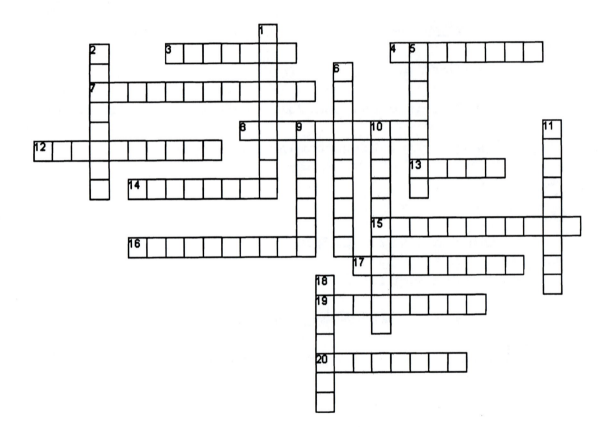

ACROSS

3. The girl's name, Colleen, is _____ from the Irish language word for girl.
4. Karen's _____ from surgery was fast.
7. He doesn't love her; _____ , he got married.
8. A professor set the _____ of our experiment.
12. The desire for a good job was her _____ to do her best in college.
13. Our class has a _____ of 2 males to 1 female.
14. The actor _____ his secret plan to marry.
15. A person in jail has many _____ on his freedom.
16. They _____ the car crash to the icy roads.
17. Women's right to vote required an _____ .
19. Many trucks on I35 _____ goods to the US.
20. The elderly often feel _____ at home alone.

DOWN

1. Electrical energy is _____ by Niagara Falls.
2. The brothers had a _____ over their inheritance.
5. _____ to AIDS could be fatal.
6. _____ causes of depression can be chemical imbalances in the body.
9. He wore a ring, so she _____ he was married.
10. Police handle the _____ of traffic laws.
11. We watched the flocks of geese in _____ from Canada to Mexico.
18. He forgot to pay his _____ bill, so he has no lights in his home.

UNIT 2

WORDS

adult	decade	guarantee	minimize
aid	deny	highlight	random
appreciation	eliminate	identical	schedule
capable	equipment	infer	solely
cooperative	gender	media	thesis

READINGS

Equal Rights
Whose Fault?
Back to School
A Tight Schedule

STRATEGIES AND SKILLS

Word Forms
- Word family chart
- Word form selection

Comprehension Check
- Matching definitions
- Identifying synonyms
- Understanding and using words in context

Word Expansion
- Multiple meaning

Interactive Speaking Practice
- Listing
- Discussion

ACADEMIC WORD POWER

LESSON 1

A. WORD FAMILIES

Study the five word families below. Then fill in the word form chart. The underlined word forms at the top of the list are the most commonly used forms in academic texts.

capable	deny	gender	guarantee (2X)	solely
/ˈkeɪpəbəl/	/dɪˈnaɪ/	/ˈgɛndər/	/gærənˈti/	/ˈsoʊli/
capability	denial		guaranteed	sole
incapable	deniable			
	undeniable			

Exercise - Word Form Chart

NOUN	VERB	ADJECTIVE	ADVERB
1.		1. capable 2.	
1.	1. deny	1. 2.	
1. gender			
1.	1. guarantee	1.	
		1.	1. solely

B. READING

Equal Rights

U.S. employers must <u>guarantee</u> equal opportunity to all potential employees who are <u>capable</u> of doing an advertised job. They cannot <u>deny</u> employment to a person based <u>solely</u> on <u>gender</u>, race, or religion. For example, in the United States, it's illegal to refuse to hire a woman for fear she'll work fewer hours because of family commitments.

C. COMPREHENSION CHECK
Exercise 1

Refer to the reading above and use the context to guess the meanings of the words below. Then match the words to their definitions. Do NOT use a dictionary.

___ 1. capable   A. to assume responsibility for, promise

___ 2. deny   B. the classification of male and female

___ 3. gender   C. refuse to give

___ 4. guarantee   D. having the ability to do something

___ 5. solely   E. alone, individually

Exercise 2

Which word does not belong?

1. capable	qualified	competent	lazy
2. deny	not allow	agree	forbid
3. guarantee	argue	promise	pledge
4. solely	together	singly	only
5. male	race	gender	sex

D. WORD STUDY
Exercise

Deny can be used in the following ways:

> 1. deny – say that something is not true
>
> 2. deny – refuse permission; reject

Read the following statements using **deny**. Decide which meaning of **deny** is used in each case. Put 1 or 2 in the blank.

___ 1. I <u>denied</u> my daughter permission to go to the party.

___ 2. The student <u>denied</u> that he had been cheating.

___ 3. The computer will <u>deny</u> me access if I don't remember my password.

___ 4. The student <u>denied</u> that she knew the teacher.

___ 5. The student's application for a work visa was <u>denied</u>.

E. USING WORDS IN COMMUNICATION

Exercise 1

1. List three things you are **not** capable of.
2. List three things you would deny your teenage children permission to do.
3. List three jobs you think are gender specific.
4. List three items you own that have a guarantee.
5. List three decisions you should not base solely on emotions.

Exercise 2

With a partner, discuss the following questions.

1. What do you think are the main differences between the two genders?
2. Did your parents deny you anything in your adolescent years?
3. What guarantee do you wish life could offer you?
4. What decisions are solely yours to make? What decisions do you make with your parents or spouse?
5. What do you wish you were capable of doing?

LESSON 2

A. WORD FAMILIES

Study the five word families below. Then fill in the word form chart. The underlined word forms at the top of the list are the most commonly used forms in academic texts.

decade	eliminate	equipment	media	minimize
/'dɛkeid/	/ɪ'lɪmə,neɪt/	/i'kwɪpmənt/	/'midiə/	/'mɪnə,maiz/
	elimination	equip		

Exercise - Word Form Chart

NOUN	VERB	ADJECTIVE	ADVERB
1. decade			
1.	1. eliminate		
1. equipment	1.		
1. media			
	1. minimize		

B. READING

Whose Fault?

When accidents affect the public, people want to know why the accidents happen so that fault can be determined. After an explosion at an electric company left some employees injured and the public without power for days, the public demanded an explanation. The president of the electric company <u>minimized</u> its role in the explosion. The <u>media</u>, however, were quick to reveal that in the last two <u>decades</u>, the company had failed to <u>eliminate</u> and replace old <u>equipment</u>, which caused the serious overload that led to the explosion. Machinery that is more than 20 years old loses its ability to function well. Since this is common knowledge in the industry, the company was negligent and therefore responsible.

C. COMPREHENSION CHECK
Exercise 1
Refer to the previous reading and use the context to guess the meanings of the words below. Then match the words to their definitions. Do NOT use a dictionary.

___ 1. decades   A. combination of TV, radio, news magazines, newspapers
___ 2. eliminate   B. useful items needed for a purpose
___ 3. equipment   C. made to seem unimportant, reduced to the limit
___ 4. media   D. to remove, to get rid of, to remove from consideration
___ 5. minimized   E. periods of 10 years

Exercise 2
True or False? Write T or F in the blanks provided.

___ 1. Governments often must <u>minimize</u> their budgets when the economy is not healthy.

___ 2. Children do not change much in their first <u>decade</u> of life.

___ 3. A profession requiring a lot of <u>equipment</u> is that of a mechanic.

___ 4. What we read in the <u>media</u> is always true.

___ 5. If a company is <u>eliminating</u> jobs, it is a good time to apply for work at that company.

D. WORD STUDY
Exercise

The verb **equip** can mean to prepare someone with the needed tools for a job. This is a **CONCRETE** meaning of the word.

It can also mean to prepare someone in terms of the knowledge or experience needed for the job. This is an **ABSTRACT** meaning of the word.

Mark the following sentences with either a C for the concrete meaning, or an A for the abstract meaning of the verb <u>equip</u>.

___ 1. The student's campus job in the computer lab <u>equipped</u> him for his future major in business computer information systems.

___ 2. Growing up in both the United States and France <u>equipped</u> the ambassador for his role as a representative of one government to the other.

___ 3. She was <u>equipped</u> for the cold Siberian winters with a down jacket, a wool hat and gloves, long underwear, and fur-lined boots.

___ 4. The U.S. soldiers in WWII were not well-<u>equipped</u> for the wet and cold winter months they spent in foxholes. Many of them suffered from trenchfoot, a disease caused by having wet feet for a long period of time.

E. USING WORDS IN COMMUNICATION
Exercise
In a group of 3 to 4 students, discuss the following.

1. If your younger sibling wanted to study abroad, what advice would you give to equip him/her for the challenge?
2. In the last decade, what historical event do you think was the most significant internationally?
3. What equipment would you need for a camping trip?
4. What primary form of the media do you rely on to inform you of current events?
5. What problem in the world do you wish you could eliminate?

LESSON 3

A. WORD FAMILIES
Study the five word families below. Then fill in the word form chart. The underlined word forms at the top of the list are the most commonly used forms in academic texts.

adult	aid (2X)	appreciation	identical	infer
/əˈdʌlt/	/eɪd/	/əˌprɪʃiˈeɪʃən/	/aɪˈdɛntəkəl/	/ɪnˈfɜr/
adulthood		appreciate	identically	inference
		appreciative		
		appreciable		
		appreciably		
		appreciated		
		unappreciated		

Exercise - Word Form Chart

NOUN	VERB	ADJECTIVE	ADVERB
1. adult 2.			
1.	1. aid		
1. appreciation	1.	1. 2. 3. 4.	1.
		1. identical	1.
1.	1. infer		

B. READING

Back to School

Adults who return to college after years of working and raising a family have a new appreciation for the pressures the young people of today face. Before returning to school, these same adults may have inferred that the pressures and challenges of today are identical to those they faced when they were young college students. Now, however, they have a better understanding of the problems and also an idea of how to aid young people with those problems.

C. COMPREHENSION CHECK
Exercise 1
Refer to the reading above and use the context to guess the meanings of the words below. Then match the words to their definitions. Do NOT use a dictionary.

____ 1. adults   A. to help physically or financially
____ 2. aid   B. people who are physically and mentally mature
____ 3. appreciation   C. gratitude, thankfulness; understanding, esteem for
____ 4. identical   D. exactly the same
____ 5. inferred   E. concluded based on some information given

Exercise 2
Choose a word from these five words in this lesson:

adult   aid   appreciation   identical   infer

1. People who are over the age of 18 are considered _____.
2. When two siblings share the same DNA, they are _____ twins.
3. Often when a country's citizens experience a natural disaster of some kind, people will even come from other countries to _____ them.
4. Even though the politicians' opinion was not stated, it can be _____ .
5. Although her field of study was engineering, she also had an _____ for the fine arts.

D. WORD STUDY
Exercise
Appreciation can be used to mean the following 4 things:

> 1. appreciation (n) - thankfulness
> 2. appreciation (n) - understanding or sympathy for
> 3. appreciation (n) - esteem for the beauty or complexity of something
> 4. appreciation (n) - increase in value

Read the following sentences using **appreciation**. Decide which meaning is used in each case, and write that number in the blank.

____ 1. Their home doubled in <u>appreciation</u> in the last five years.

____ 2. The teacher developed a new <u>appreciation</u> for her language students when she moved to the Ukraine and struggled with learning Ukrainian.

____ 3. A successful Thai businessman showed his <u>appreciation</u> for his education at a U.S. university by giving a generous donation to its business school.

____ 4. Studying the solar system gave the students a new <u>appreciation</u> of the vastness of the universe.

E. USING WORDS IN COMMUNICATION
Exercise
In a group of 3 or 4 students, discuss the following questions.

1. Name three things that can be <u>identical</u>.

2. Who are the three most influential <u>adults</u> in your life?

3. What kind of <u>aid</u> have you received?

4. What kind of <u>aid</u> have you given to others?

5. Have you <u>inferred</u> something about someone and later discovered that it was not true?

6. How do you show <u>appreciation</u> to someone who has helped you in a significant way?

LESSON 4

A. WORD FAMILIES

Study the five word families below. Then fill in the word form chart. The underlined word forms at the top of the list are the most commonly used forms in academic texts.

cooperative	highlight (2X)	random	schedule (2X)	thesis
/koʊˈɑprətɪv/	/ˈhaɪˌlaɪt/	/ˈrændəm/	/ˈskɛdʒul/	/ˈθisəs/
cooperate		randomly	scheduled	
cooperation		randomness	rescheduled	
cooperatively			unscheduled	

Exercise - Word Form Chart

NOUN	VERB	ADJECTIVE	ADVERB
1.	1.	1. cooperative	1.
1.	1. highlight		
1.		1. random	1.
1. schedule	1.	1. 2. 3.	
1. thesis			

B. READING

A Tight Schedule

The doctoral student compared his work <u>schedule</u> and his class schedule carefully. Then he <u>highlighted</u> all the times he would have available to work on his research <u>thesis</u>. He knew that using a <u>random</u> hour here and there would not be enough to complete the research needed. Fortunately, his boss was <u>cooperative</u> and allowed him to set his own schedule.

C. COMPREHENSION CHECK
Exercise 1
Refer to the reading above and use the context to guess the meanings of the words below. Then match the words to their definitions. Do NOT use a dictionary.

___ 1. cooperative   A. marked for emphasis
___ 2. highlighted   B. willing to do what is needed or asked
___ 3. random   C. an argument or theory; a graduate research paper
___ 4. schedule   D. happening at any time; unplanned
___ 5. thesis   E. a list of timed planned events

Exercise 2

Choose the word from the word form chart that belongs in each blank.

1. The other professors argued with his _____ that anxiety helped students perform better on tests.
2. As she studied, she _____ points in her textbook.
3. If a person is willing to do what is asked, he is _____
4. A _____ *Walk Down Wall Street*, a book on investing in the stock market, suggests that readers pick which stocks to invest in by throwing darts at a chart rather than carefully examining their previous records.
5. The medical intern had such a full work _____ that he had no time to sleep.

D. WORD STUDY
Exercise
Highlight can be used in these ways:

1. highlight (v) - in the literal sense of using a highlighter pen to mark a text for emphasis.
2. highlight (v) - in the verbal/visual sense when referring to a speaker's use of voice emphasis, hand gestures, charts, diagrams, etc.
3. highlight (n) - a positive, memorable event.

Read the following sentences and decide what meaning is expressed. Write 1, 2, or 3 on the line provided.

___ 1. The diagram <u>highlighted</u> the difference between the incidence of cancer in smokers and non-smokers.
___ 2. The <u>highlight</u> of our trip to India was staying in the home of a former classmate.
___ 3. The used book I purchased had all the key points <u>highlighted</u>.
___ 4. Our teacher <u>highlighted</u> the importance of doing all our homework.

E. USING WORDS IN COMMUNICATION
Exercise
With a partner, read and discuss the following.

1. Describe a <u>highlight</u> of a trip you took.
2. Describe a <u>cooperative</u> student.
3. Describe a <u>random</u> event in your life that brought you joy.
4. Describe your usual <u>schedule</u>.
5. Do you agree with the <u>thesis</u> that if you study hard, you can learn anything? Why or why not?

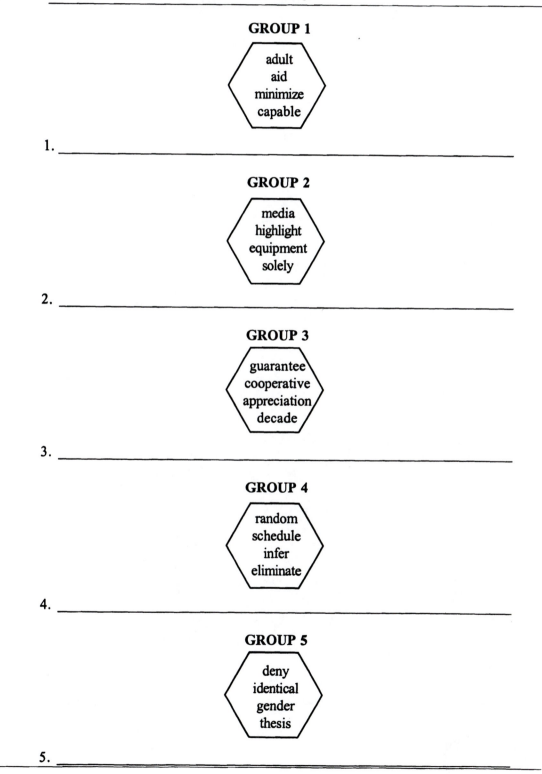

REVIEW
Write original sentences using the vocabulary words in each group. For each group, write one sentence using **two** vocabulary words for a total of five original sentences. Add as many words necessary to make a complete, sensible sentence. Compare your sentences with a partner and discuss meanings.

GROUP 1

adult
aid
minimize
capable

1. _____

GROUP 2

media
highlight
equipment
solely

2. _____

GROUP 3

guarantee
cooperative
appreciation
decade

3. _____

GROUP 4

random
schedule
infer
eliminate

4. _____

GROUP 5

deny
identical
gender
thesis

5. _____

UNIT 3

WORDS

abstract	diversity	guidelines	prior
automatically	enhance	innovation	quotation
bias	exceed	inspection	restore
confirm	foundation	neutral	successive
contemporary	global	precede	unique

READINGS

Pollution from Cars
Multicultural Matters
Structural Trouble
Artistic Changes

STRATEGIES AND SKILLS

Word Forms
- □ Word family chart
- □ Word form selection

Comprehension Check
- □ Matching definitions
- □ Identifying and using words in context
- □ Identifying synonyms

Word Expansion
- □ Multiple meaning
- □ Suffixes

Interactive Speaking Practice
- □ Sentence completion
- □ Associations
- □ Listing

ACADEMIC WORD POWER

LESSON 1

A. WORD FAMILIES
Study the five word families below. Then fill in the word form chart. The underlined word forms at the top of the list are the most commonly used forms in academic texts.

automatically	confirm	exceed	guidelines	inspection
/ɔtə'mætɪkli/	/kən'fɜrm/	/ɪk'sid/	/'gaɪd,laɪnz/	/ɪn'spɛkʃən/
automate	confirmation	exceedingly		inspect
automatic				inspected
automated				inspector
automation				

Exercise - Word Form Chart

NOUN	VERB	ADJECTIVE	ADVERB
1.	1.	1. 2.	1. automatically
1.	1. confirm		
	1. exceed		1.
1. guidelines			
1. inspection 2.	1.	1.	

B. READING
Pollution from Cars

Automobile safety <u>inspection</u> <u>guidelines</u> state that a car with high levels of pollutants in the exhaust system would <u>automatically</u> fail. My old car's inspection <u>confirmed</u> my fears that its pollutants would <u>exceed</u> the acceptable limit. Since my old car did not meet the guidelines, I must get my car repaired or get a new one.

C. COMPREHENSION CHECK
Exercise 1
Refer to the reading above and use the context to guess the meanings of the words below. Then match the words to their definitions. Do NOT use a dictionary.

____	1. automatically	A.	a close, careful look
____	2. confirmed	B.	certain to happen
____	3. exceed	C.	to be more than expected, to do or say more than is needed
____	4. guidelines	D.	ideas or rules of what to do, or not to do
____	5. inspection	E.	reinforced; made sure of something by checking again

Exercise 2

Choose a word from this lesson to fill in the blanks below.

1. The top students usually _____ the requirements of a course.
2. Before moving to a foreign country, it is a good idea to read some _____ on socially acceptable behavior in the new culture.
3. Calculators can _____ calculate the square root of a number.
4. Upon careful _____ of my computer program assignment, I discovered a flaw in its design.
5. We _____ all of our measurements before calculating the data.

D. WORD STUDY

Exercise

Consider these different meanings of the word **confirm**.

> 1. confirm (v) - to check something again to be sure it is correct
>
> 2. confirm (v) - to make something legal or formally accepted
>
> 3. confirmed (adj) - settled in certain habits or state of health

Read the following sentences and decide which meaning of **confirm** is being used. Write 1, 2, or 3 in the blank.

___ 1. The Senate will <u>confirm</u> the judge in a ceremony at the Supreme Court today.
___ 2. My literature professor is a <u>confirmed</u> bachelor.
___ 3. The results of the physics experiment <u>confirmed</u> the theory they had studied.
___ 4. The story that the president of the university is taking a new job at a larger university in another state has not been <u>confirmed</u>.
___ 5. I need to <u>confirm</u> my flight and hotel reservation the day before I leave on my trip.

E. USING WORDS IN COMMUNICATION

Exercise

Repeat and complete the following sentences.

1. Because of my parents' <u>guidelines</u>...
2. The city streetlights <u>automatically</u> ...
3. The admissions office <u>inspected</u>...
4. The student <u>exceeded</u> her parents' expectations when she...
5. The exam score <u>confirmed</u>...

Lesson 2

A. WORD FAMILIES

Study the five word families below. Then fill in the word form chart. The underlined word forms at the top of the list are the most commonly used forms in academic texts.

bias	contemporary (2X)	diversity	enhance	global
/'baɪəs/	/kən'tempər,eri/	/dɪ'vɜrsɪti/	/ɛn'hæns/	/'gloʊbəl/
biased		diverse	enhanced	globe
unbiased		diversify	enhancement	globally
		diversely		globalization
		diversified		
		diversifying		
		diversification		

Exercise - Word Form Chart

NOUN	VERB	ADJECTIVE	ADVERB
1. bias		1. 2.	
1.		1. contemporary	
1. diversity 2.	1.	1. 2. 3.	1.
1.	1. enhance	1.	
1. 2.		1. global	1.

B. READING

Multicultural Matters

A <u>contemporary</u> issue in most university admissions offices is to achieve a student body with <u>global</u> <u>diversity</u>. Educators believe that a student's education is <u>enhanced</u> through exposure to all kinds of races, beliefs, cultures, etc. This exposure helps reduce any cultural <u>bias</u> or ignorance a student may have. Therefore, diversifying the student body is a worthy goal.

C. COMPREHENSION CHECK
Exercise 1

Refer to the reading above and use the context to guess the meanings of the words below. Then match the words to their definitions. Do NOT use a dictionary.

___ 1. bias
___ 2. contemporary
___ 3. diversity
___ 4. enhanced
___ 5. global

A. a variety, differences among people
B. a general tendency, prejudice
C. relating to all the world
D. improved, added to
E. of today, modern

Exercise 2

Write YES if the word from the above list is used correctly and NO if it is not.

_____ 1. We added additional RAM to our computer, and it greatly <u>enhanced</u> its performance.

_____ 2. William Faulkner, a famous American author, lived in a small Mississippi town and wrote most of his novels and short stories about life in that area. He had a very <u>global</u> perspective.

_____ 3. Coal is a <u>contemporary</u> source of heat in modern homes.

_____ 4. Fashion designers seem to have a <u>bias</u> toward thin people. All the clothes look the best on them.

_____ 5. If a class has students from seven different countries, there is not much <u>diversity</u>.

D. WORD STUDY
Exercise

The word **contemporary** is an adjective, but it can also be used as a noun meaning someone of the same age or of the same time period.

Choose whether the adjective or the noun form is used in each of the sentences below. Write A for adjective and N for noun.

___ 1. A famous author of fantasy, J. R. R. Tolkien, was a <u>contemporary</u> of C. S. Lewis, who also wrote imaginative fantasy novels.

___ 2. An interior design major, Yosuke decorated his apartment in a very <u>contemporary</u> style.

___ 3. The Department of Veteran Affairs estimated that as of 1999, World War II veterans and their <u>contemporaries</u> were dying at a rate of 1,038 per day, 31,600 per month, and 379,000 per year. That rate accelerates monthly.

___ 4. The terms **recycle** and **made from recycled paper** are <u>contemporary</u> to our generation.

E. USING WORDS IN COMMUNICATION

Exercise 1

Word Associations - In the chart below, write one word you associate with each of the words from this lesson. Then go around the classroom and see if anyone has one or more of the same words associated with the vocabulary words. If you find someone who does, sit with that classmate and discuss your associations. If you do not find a student with any of the same associations, choose a partner with whom to discuss your associations.

bias	
contemporary	
diversity	
enhanced	
global	

Exercise 2

With the same partner from the exercise above, discuss these questions.

1. Tell about one <u>bias</u> that you have.

2. Do you see any obvious <u>biases</u> in the other cultures you have been exposed to?

3. What is an important <u>contemporary</u> issue in the world today?

4. How much <u>diversity</u> did you experience in your hometown?

5. How could living in a foreign country <u>enhance</u> your education?

6. What <u>global</u> issue concerns you?

LESSON 3

A. WORD FAMILIES

Study the five word families below. Then fill in the word form chart. The underlined word forms at the top of the list are the most commonly used forms in academic texts.

foundation
/fɑʊnˈdeɪʃən/
founder

quotation
/kwoʊˈteɪʃən/
quote (2X)

innovation
/ˌɪnəˈveɪʃən/
innovate
innovative
innovator

prior (2X)
/ˈpraɪər/

restore
/rəˈstɔr/
restored
restoration

Exercise - Word Form Chart

NOUN	VERB	ADJECTIVE	ADVERB
1. foundation 2.			
1. quotation 2.	1.		
1. innovation 2.	1.	1.	
		1.	1. prior (to)*
1.	1. restore	1.	

* **prior to** is a prepositional phrase that is used as an adverb

B. READING

Structural Trouble

Prior to making an offer to purchase the building, we had discovered that its foundation had shifted in the clay soil. We consulted an engineer for a neutral opinion on whether it could be repaired. This was followed by consulting a construction contractor, who gave a price quotation of $5,000 to restore the building using the latest innovation for this type of work. Based on this information, we decided not to make an offer.

C. COMPREHENSION CHECK
Exercise 1
Refer to the reading above and use the context to guess the meanings of the words below.
Then match the words to their definitions. Do NOT use a dictionary.

___ 1. foundation   A. a statement of price; a small part taken from
                   something longer (a book, play, speech, etc.)

___ 2. quotation   B. to make something look like it did when it was new

___ 3. innovation   C. earlier, previous

___ 4. prior   D. the base on which a structure or system of belief is built

___ 5. restore   E. something newly made or improved with creativity.

Exercise 2
Choose a word from the five listed above.

1. The professor used a _____ from my favorite author in her lecture.

2. It is a huge project to _____ the oldest building on campus. The historical society has researched exactly how the building looked when it was new and plans to follow the original plan exactly.

3. It is difficult, both academically and financially, to keep up with every _____ in the computer field.

4. American democracy is built on the _____ of a system of checks and balances designed so that one person or branch of the government cannot take control of the nation.

5. There are numerous prerequisites that I am required to take _____ to registering for the class in which I am most interested.

D. WORD STUDY
Exercise
The word **foundation** and its other word forms can have these meanings:

1. foundation - the physical base something is built on (physical meaning)
2. foundation - the philosophical base on which a system of belief or an institution is built (abstract meaning)
3. foundation - an organization, usually nonprofit, which provides money for projects in the arts, sciences, and education (organizational meaning)
4. founded - started or begun
5. founder - refers to a person who establishes something, such as a college, a business, a church, or a social movement.

Write the number of the correct meaning of the word in the blank in front of the following sentences.

___ 1. The _____ of Rice University in Houston, Texas was William Marsh Rice.

___ 2. The _____ of the United States government is participatory democracy.

___ 3. Sigmund Freud was the _____ of psychoanalysis.

___ 4. The Frank Lloyd Wright _____ maintains this famous architect's home in Oak Park, Illinois as a historic house museum.

___ 5. The scientific _____ of the space program began over a century ago.

___ 6. A _____ of poured cement is the norm in home construction in Texas.

___ 7. In 1979, Rice University School of Social Sciences was _____ .

E. USING WORDS IN COMMUNICATION
Exercise

1. List 3 <u>innovations</u> that you use daily.

2. List 3 things you had to do <u>prior</u> to coming to school today.

3. List 3 <u>foundations</u> of your belief system.

4. List 3 things you wish you could <u>restore</u>.

5. Give 3 <u>quotations</u> by famous people.

LESSON 4

A. WORD FAMILIES

Study the five word families below. Then fill in the word form chart. The underlined word forms at the top of the list are the most commonly used forms in academic texts.

abstract (2X)	preceding	neutral	successive	unique
/æb'strækt/	/pri'sidŋ/	/'nutrəl/	/sək'sɛsiv/	/'yunik/
abstractly	precede	neutrality	successor	uniquely
abstraction	precedent	neutralize	succession	uniqueness
	precedence	neutralization	successively	
	unprecedented			

Exercise - Word Form Chart

NOUN	VERB	ADJECTIVE	ADVERB
1. 2.		1. abstract	1.
1. 2.	1.	1. preceding 2.	
1. 2.	1.	1. neutral	
1. 2.		1. successive	1.
1.		1. unique	1.

B. READING

Artistic Changes

The artist's latest paintings were <u>unique</u> and <u>abstract</u>. Prior to his graduate studies, he had painted in a realistic style and primarily used <u>neutral</u> colors, but in his later works, each <u>successive</u> painting was more vibrant and unusual than the <u>preceding</u> one.

C. COMPREHENSION CHECK
Exercise 1
Refer to the reading above and use the context to guess the meanings of the words below. Then match the words to their definitions. Do NOT use a dictionary.

___ 1. abstract   A. coming before something

___ 2. preceding   B. dull in color

___ 3. neutral   C. unclear, vague, related to ideas or feelings

___ 4. successive   D. one of a kind, without equal

___ 5. unique   E. following after another

Exercise 2
Circle the word that is not related to the first word of each line below.

1. abstract	confusing	concrete	conceptual
2. neutral	dull	vibrant	indefinite
3. unique	unusual	singular	similar
4. preceding	preference	preliminary	former
5. successive	following	successful	sequential

D. WORD STUDY
Exercise 1
Neutral can have these meanings:

> 1. neutral - impartial, not on either side of a disagreement or issue
>
> 2. neutral - as related to colors: dull, indefinite

Choose which form of **neutral** belongs in the sentences below.

1. My professor for world religions did an amazing job of maintaining her _____ in her presentations of the world religions. At the end of the course, all of the students were curious to know if she was a believer in any of them.
     a. neutralize   b. neutrality   c. neutral

2. Switzerland was a _____ nation in WW II.
     a. neutralize   b. neutrality   c. neutral

3. Journalists are required to present their stories with _____ .
     a. neutralize   b. neutrality   c. neutral

4. Larry doesn't like to stand out in a crowd, so he tends to choose _____ shades for his shirts and pants.
     a. neutralize   b. neutrality   c. neutral

Exercise 2
Abstract can have these meanings:

> 1. abstract (n) - a brief summary of an article or academic paper
>
> 2. abstract (n) - a powder made from a drug (pharmaceutical meaning)
>
> 3. abstract (adj) - vague, unclear
>
> 4. abstract (adj) - not concrete, related to ideas
>
> 5. abstract (v) - to remove, to draw out, to separate
>
> 6. abstract (v) - to summarize, to shorten

Read the following sentences and write the number from the above explanations that corresponds to the meaning of the vocabulary word.

_____ 1. I am so practical that philosophy is too <u>abstract</u> for me to process.

_____ 2. The dentist <u>abstracted</u> the infected tooth.

_____ 3. He used an <u>abstract</u> of extropipate to make this pain reliever.

_____ 4. The deadline for the <u>abstract</u> of your research paper is Friday at noon.

_____ 5. I <u>abstracted</u> my favorite lines of the poem and used them as the topic of my poetry paper.

_____ 6. Do these directions tell me to do this reading first and then do the experiment? They are so <u>abstract</u>, I am not sure.

E. USING WORDS IN COMMUNICATION
Exercise
With a partner, discuss these questions.

1. Describe a <u>unique</u> friend of yours.

2. What issue are you NOT <u>neutral</u> about?

3. What are some things you did (or hope to do) in the year <u>preceding</u> your graduation from high school?

4. What plans do you have for the year <u>successive</u> to this one?

5. How would you define the <u>abstract</u> words **beauty** and **honor**?

REVIEW

Write the letter of the sentence that corresponds with the word from this unit.

___ 1. abstract   a. A class with _____ has different kinds of people.

___ 2. automatically   b. A new invention is an _____ .

___ 3. bias   c. Houses are built on a _____ .

___ 4. confirmed   d. If something is not concrete, it is _____ .

___ 5. contemporary   e. If someone is of the same time period as you,
                          he is your _____ .

___ 6. diversity   f. If something is better than you expect, it _____ your
                          expectations.

___ 7. enhanced   g. If something works by itself it works _____ .
___ 8. exceeds   h. If you are one of a kind, you are _____ .

___ 9. foundation   i. If you aren't for or against something, you are _____ .

___ 10. global   j. If you called the airline to check on your flight, you
                          _____ it.

___ 11. guidelines   k. If you do something before you go home, it is done
                          _____ to going home.

___ 12. innovation   l. If you have a prejudice, you have a _____ .

___ 13. inspection   m. If you make something better, it is _____ .

___ 14. neutral   n. The day before today was the _____ one.

___ 15. preceding   o. To fix something so it looks new again is to _____ it.

___ 16. prior   p. To use someone else's words is to use a _____ .

___ 17. quotation   q. Today's economy is _____ . It affects the entire
                          world.

___ 18. restore   r. Yesterday, today, and tomorrow are _____ days.

___ 19. successive   s. You give an _____ when you give a careful look at
                          something.

___ 20. unique   t. Your teachers give you _____ to help you succeed.

UNIT 4

WORDS

acknowledge	conformity	intervention	simulation
advocate	crucial	mode	somewhat
ambiguous	discrimination	phenomenon	tension
cite	dynamic	presumption	transformation
comprehensive	eventually	rational	widespread

READINGS

A Good Roommate
To Be a Master
Age Discrimination
Her Best Face Forward

STRATEGIES AND SKILLS

Word Forms
- ▫ Word family chart
- ▫ Word form selection

Comprehension Check
- ▫ Matching definitions
- ▫ Understanding and using words in context
- ▫ Pairing sentence halves
- ▫ Identifying synonyms

Word Expansion
- ▫ Idiomatic usage
- ▫ Multiple meanings
- ▫ Usage in specific domains
- ▫ Grammar applications
- ▫ Identifying antonyms

Interactive Speaking Practice
- ▫ Listing
- ▫ Role play
- ▫ Sentence completion

ACADEMIC WORD POWER

LESSON 1

A. WORD FAMILIES
Study the five word families below. Then fill in the word form chart. The underlined word forms at the top of the list are the most commonly used forms in academic texts.

tension	intervention	advocate (2X)	acknowledge	cite
/ˈtenʃən/	/ɪntərˈvenʃən/	/ˈædvəkɪt/	/ɪkˈnɑlɪdʒ/	/ˈsaɪt/
tense (2X)	intervene	advocacy	acknowledgement	cited
tensely				citation

Exercise - Word Form Chart

NOUN	VERB	ADJECTIVE	ADVERB
1. tension	1.	1.	1.
1. intervention	1.		
1. advocate 2.	1.		
1.	1. acknowledge		
1.	1. cite	1.	

B. READING

A Good Roommate

Jeremy's roommate, Andrew, was an <u>advocate</u> for Alcoholics Anonymous (AA), an organization that helps people who can't control their drinking. When he became concerned about Jeremy's drinking problem, Andrew felt some kind of <u>intervention</u> was called for to stop Jeremy's destructive behavior. He arranged a meeting between Jeremy and his family and friends. <u>Tension</u> filled the room as they all took turns and <u>cited</u> examples of the severity of the problem. Eventually, Jeremy <u>acknowledged</u> that he did indeed have a problem and that he needed help. According to Alcoholics Anonymous, this is the first step toward recovery.

C. COMPREHENSION CHECK
Exercise 1
Refer to the reading above and use the context to guess the meanings of the words below.
Then match the words to their definitions. Do NOT use a dictionary.

____ 1. tension   A. recognized

____ 2. intervention   B. a worker for a cause

____ 3. advocate   C. doing something to try to stop a problem

____ 4. acknowledged   D. a state of stress; tautness

____ 5. cited   E. mentioned or quoted as an example

Exercise 2
Read the following sentences. If the underlined word is used correctly, write YES in the blank, and NO if it is not.

_____ 1. We have <u>tension</u> in our lives when we have many exams.

_____ 2. We are <u>advocates</u> for the right to drink while driving if we are members of Alcoholics Anonymous. (Refer to the reading above to see what AA is.)

_____ 3. If a professor does not call on you to answer a question, she has <u>acknowledged</u> your raised hand.

_____ 4. The teacher <u>cited</u> your perfect attendance record as evidence that you were not a serious student.

_____ 5. NAFSA, an Association of International Educators, is an <u>advocate</u> for international student programs.

_____ 6. Ralph Nader, a well-known consumer <u>advocate</u>, is concerned with product safety and fair advertising practices.

_____ 7. Demonstrators against a military <u>intervention</u> would support a war.

D. WORD STUDY
Exercise 1
Play the devil's advocate is an expression used to mean someone who argues an opposing position to stimulate argument. Other people in the same setting may not know for sure whether a person is playing devil's advocate or if that person really has the view he or she is presenting. Example: In our class discussion on women's right to equal pay for equal work, everyone was for equal pay. Therefore, Marco was assigned the role of devil's advocate. He argued vehemently against equal pay for equal work.

Circle the choices that complete the following sentence correctly.
(There are 3 correct answers.)

Someone could be playing the <u>devil's advocate</u> when he:
   a. argues against his own proposal.
   b. asks questions he knows the answers to.
   c. argues for something clearly evil.
   d. is not a good person.
   e. takes the opposite side of the majority view in a group discussion.
   f. gets in a fist fight with another member in a debate.

Exercise 2

Consider these different meanings of the word **cite**.

> 1. cite (v) - to mention or quote as an example
>
> 2. cite (v) - to issue a legal summons
>
> 3. cite (v) - to honor someone officially

Read the following sentences and decide which meaning of cite is used. Write the corresponding number on the line.

___ 1. A policeman <u>cited</u> him for drunk driving. He received a citation to appear in court next month.

___ 2. The director of student housing was <u>cited</u> for her extraordinary service to students. She often invited those students who stayed in the dormitories over holidays to her home for a meal.

___ 3. In a research paper, you should <u>cite</u> the work of authorities in the field of your topic.

___ 4. The Congressional Medal of Honor recipients were <u>cited</u> in a ceremony at the White House.

E. USING WORDS IN COMMUNICATION
Exercise
Read and discuss these questions with a partner.

1. For what cause could you be an <u>advocate</u>?

2. What causes <u>tension</u> in your life?

3. Has anyone <u>intervened</u> in your life at a time when you needed it? Have you ever <u>intervened</u> in the life of a friend? Is there someone you know who needs some <u>intervention</u> in their life now?

4. Have you ever had the experience that someone does not a<u>cknowledge</u> your presence? If so, how did it make you feel?

5. What examples might you <u>cite</u> to show that your best friend is worthy of your friendship?

LESSON 2

A. WORD FAMILIES

Study the five word families below. Then fill in the word form chart. The underlined word forms at the top of the list are the most commonly used forms in academic texts.

crucial	comprehensive	rational	presumption	widespread
/ˈkruʃəl/	/ˌkɑmpriˈhɛnsiv/	/ˈræʃənəl/	/priˈzʌmpʃən/	/ˈwaɪdˌsprɛd/
crucially	comprehensively	irrational	presume	
		rationally	presumptuous	
		rationality		
		rationalize		
		rationalism		
		rationalization		

Exercise - Word Form Chart

NOUN	VERB	ADJECTIVE	ADVERB
		1. crucial	1.
		1. comprehensive	1.
1. 2. 3.	1.	1. rational 2.	1.
1. presumption	1.	1.	
		1. widespread	

B. READING

To Be a Master

It is crucial for graduate students to pass a comprehensive exam over all their preceding course work. These exams contribute to widespread stress and extreme anxiety. Many students feel it is an unreasonable demand, but there is a rational explanation for the requirement. The university has the presumption that "masters" of any subject should have a broad understanding of their field.

C. COMPREHENSION CHECK
Exercise 1
Refer to the reading above and use the context to guess the meanings of the words below. Then match the words to their definitions. Do NOT use a dictionary.

_____ 1. crucial   A. reasonable, sensible, logical
_____ 2. comprehensive   B. the thinking that something is true
_____ 3. rational   C. extremely important
_____ 4. presumption   D. that which includes everything
_____ 5. widespread   E. covering a large area

Exercise 2
Fill in the blanks with the correct word from this lesson.

1. Calcium is _____ for strong bones.

2. People who do not have _____ patterns of thought could have psychological problems.

3. Despite not finding conclusive evidence for this view, there has been a persistent _____ that J. F. Kennedy was killed as part of a conspiracy.

4. Long-term droughts can result in _____ devastation to the land.

5. The professor's review before the exam was _____ . The review covered all the material we had learned in class so far.

D. WORD STUDY
Exercise 1
Rationalism, rationalization, and **rationality** are all nouns but have different meanings.

> 1. **Rationalism** is a philosophy that says reason can explain all human behavior and is the source of all knowledge.
>
> 2. **Rationalization** in psychology means the giving of rational explanations or excuses for one's actions and beliefs without being aware that they are not the real motives.
>
> 3. **Rationality** is the ability to think clearly.

Choose the correct word for the sentences below.

1. Because her _____ was questioned, the nurses did not take her complaints seriously.

2. Marxism is a belief system built on _____ .

3. Psychologists tell us that there are two reasons for the things we do. One is the real reason, which is often selfish, and the other is a _____ that makes it look like we had good reason for what we did.

4. His _____ for failing two classes this semester was that he had been sick part of the time and never caught up.

Exercise 2
Find the errors in the following sentences and correct them.

1. It is <u>crucially</u> that you pay you're bills on time.   (2 mistakes)

2. He took his <u>comprehensively</u> exam on Thursday, and he past it.   (2 mistakes)

3. Patients with anorexia always <u>rationalizing</u> that they cannot eat because they are fat.

     (1 mistake)

4. The <u>presumed</u> that the professor would rise our grades because the average was so low was a faulty one.   (2 mistakes)

5. Parallel parking is a <u>crucial</u> part of a drive test.   (1 mistake)

E. USING WORDS IN COMMUNICATION
Exercise
Make lists for these sentences, and then share them with a group of 2-4 students.

1. List 3 things you think are <u>crucial</u> for success in life.

2. List 3 <u>presumptions</u> you had about the teacher of this class before you met him/her.

3. List 3 problems you consider <u>widespread</u> in the world.

4. List 3 <u>rationalizations</u> a student could give for failing a test.

LESSON 3

A. WORD FAMILIES
Study the five word families below. Then fill in the word form chart. The underlined word forms at the top of the list are the most commonly used forms in academic texts.

conformity	somewhat	ambiguous	discrimination	eventually
/kənˈfɔrmɪti/	/ˈsʌmwɑt/	/æmˈbɪgyuəs/	/dɪscrɪməˈneɪʃən/	/iˈvɛntʃuəli/
conform		ambiguity	discriminate	eventuality
conformist		unambiguous	discriminating	
conformance		ambiguously		
nonconformist		unambiguously		

Exercise - Word Form Chart

NOUN	VERB	ADJECTIVE	ADVERB
1. conformity 2. 3. 4.	1.		
			1. somewhat
1.		1. ambiguous 2.	1. 2.
1.discrimination	1.	1.	
1.			1. eventually

B. READING

Age Discrimination

A female journalist was fired from her job after 30 years of experience. Although the reasons given were somewhat ambiguous, she believed she was a victim of age discrimination. She filed a complaint. The case was reviewed, and in order to be in conformity under current anti-discrimination laws, the company eventually gave her job back to her.

C. COMPREHENSION CHECK
Exercise 1
Refer to the reading above and use the context to guess the meanings of the words below. Then match the words to their definitions. Do NOT use a dictionary.

___ 1. conformity	A.	unfair treatment
___ 2. somewhat	B.	happening later, ultimately
___ 3. ambiguous	C.	acting in the same manner as others
___ 4 discrimination	D.	to a small degree
___ 5 eventually	E.	confusing, able to be understood in different ways.

Exercise 2
Match the clauses on the left with those that complete them on the right.

___	1. If you are in <u>conformity</u> with company policy,	A. you think someone has mistreated you because of your race, beliefs, nationality, gender, etc.
___	2. If you are <u>somewhat</u> sure of an answer.	B. you do what is expected for the situation.
___	3. If you think you have been <u>discriminated</u> against,	C. you are not completely confident.
___	4. If you <u>eventually</u> do your homehomework,	D. you don't do it as soon as you get home from class.
___	5. If directions are <u>ambiguous</u>,	E. there could be more than one interpretation.

D. WORD STUDY
Exercise
Each of the statements below is an example that has an opposite meaning of one word in this lesson. Write the word that the statement is NOT an example of in the blank.
(Example: NOT <u>poor</u>   He always travels first class.)

NOT _____   1. He seemed blind to the fact that his students were rich, poor, White, Black, Hispanic, and Asian, and he treated them all the same.

NOT _____   2. The doctor answered the phone after only one ring.

NOT _____   3. She was the only student who wore dresses to gym class.

NOT _____   4. The directions on how to assemble the new computer were so clear that a child could have done it.

NOT _____   5. The professor was completely satisfied with my paper and gave me an "A".

E. USING WORDS IN COMMUNICATION
Exercise 1
Read and discuss these questions with a partner.

1. What are you <u>somewhat</u> good at?

2. What would you <u>eventually</u> like to do?

3. What <u>discrimination</u> have you ever seen or experienced?

4. Give an example of <u>conformity</u> that you have fought against.

5. How would you tell your girlfriend or boyfriend in an <u>ambiguous</u> way that you like her/him?

Exercise 2
With your partner, role play number 5 from the above list for the rest of the class.

LESSON 4

A. WORD FAMILIES

Study the five word families below. Then fill in the word form chart. The underlined word forms at the top of the list are the most commonly used forms in academic texts.

simulation	dynamic	transformation	phenomenon	mode
/sɪmyə'leɪʃən/	/daɪ'næmɪk/	/ˌtrænsfər'meɪʃə/	/fɛ'namə,nan/	/moʊd/
simulate	dynamically	transform	phenomena	
simulated	dynamics	transformed	phenomenal	

Exercise - Word Form Chart

NOUN	VERB	ADJECTIVE	ADVERB
1. simulation	1.	1.	
1.		1. dynamic	1.
1. transformation	1.	1.	
1. phenomenon 2.		1.	
1. mode			

B. READING

Her Best Face Forward

After viewing a computer <u>simulation</u> of how she would look after plastic surgery, Susan felt the <u>transformation</u> would be worth the pain and financial cost. Indeed, after the surgery, her friends thought her change of appearance was quite a <u>phenomenon</u>. Even her personality changed. She had always been a somewhat active person, but after the surgery, she became <u>dynamic</u>. She felt so good, she even decided to change her <u>mode</u> of transportation and bought a new car to go with her new appearance.

C. COMPREHENSION CHECK
Exercise 1
Refer to the reading above and use the context to guess the meanings of the words below.
Then match the words to their definitions. Do NOT use a dictionary.

___ 1. simulation	A. an imitation of a real situation
___ 2. dynamic	B. a manner or way of doing something
___ 3. transformation	C. a highly unusual event that attracts attention
___ 4. phenomenon	D. energetic, very active
___ 5. mode	E. the act of changing from one state to another

Exercise 2
Which word does not belong?

1. simulation	copy	original	facsimile
2. dynamic	dramatic	strong	peaceful
3. transformation	acceptance	change	modification
4. mode	method	style	fact
5. phenomenon	wonder	normal	marvel

D. WORD STUDY
Exercise
Study the different meanings of the word **dynamic**.

---

1. dynamic (adj) – energetic, very active

2. dynamics (n) – factors that shape a personal relationship

3. dynamics (n) – the study of force and motion

Read the following sentences and put the correct form of **dynamic** in the blank.

1. Our drama teacher is so _____, that we can't help but learn acting from her.

2. Mechanical engineering students were studying the _____ of the water wheel at the old mill.

3. The students in the graduate psychology course have to observe family therapy sessions to see family _____ in action.

4. I am concerned about my roommate's relationship with her boyfriend. Something about the _____ does not seem healthy.

E. USING WORDS IN COMMUNICATION
Exercise

In a group of 3-4 students, read and complete these sentences.

1. If I could <u>transform</u> something in my life it would be…

2. A <u>dynamic</u> person I know is…

3. My favorite <u>mode</u> of communication to my family and friends is…

4. The <u>phenomenon</u> I wish I could witness is…

5. I would like to see a <u>simulation</u> of…

REVIEW

Choose any five words from this unit and write one in each oval. Then write any four words that you associate with those words on the extending lines. Be able to explain your associations to a partner. (See the example at right.)

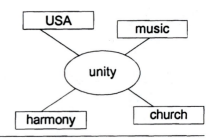

1.

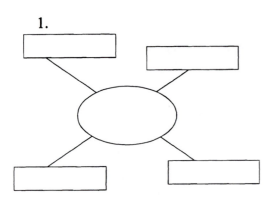

2.

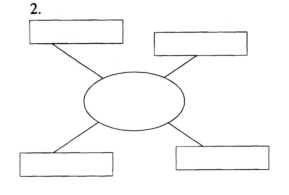

3.

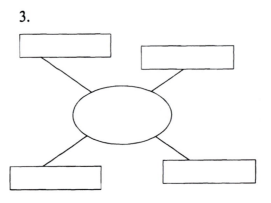

4.

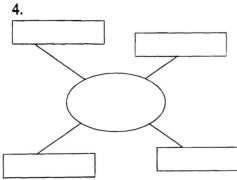

5.

UNIT 5

WORDS

aggregate	explicit	publication	topic
comprise	incentive	release	transmission
contradiction	initiative	reverse	ultimately
domain	interval	subsidiary	visible
edition	prohibit	survive	voluntary

READINGS
Batter Up
Censor the Internet?
How to Solve a Mystery
Charitable News

STRATEGIES AND SKILLS
Word Forms
- □ Word family chart
- □ Word form selection

Comprehension Check
- □ Matching definitions
- □ Understanding and using words in context
- □ Identifying synonyms

Word Expansion
- □ Multiple meaning
- □ Usage in specific domains
- □ Collocations

Interactive Speaking Practice
- □ Role Play
- □ Listing
- □ Discussion

ACADEMIC WORD POWER

LESSON 1

A. WORD FAMILIES

Study the five word families below. Then fill in the word form chart. The underlined word forms at the top of the list are the most commonly used forms in academic texts.

aggregate (2X)	domain	incentive	release (2X)	visible
/ˈægrəgɪt/	/doʊˈmein/	/ɪnˈsɛntɪv/	/riˈlis/	/ˌvɪzəˈbəl/
aggregation				visibly
				visibility
				invisibility

Exercise - Word Form Chart

NOUN	VERB	ADJECTIVE	ADVERB
1. aggregate 2.	1.		
1. domain			
1. incentive			
1.	1. release		
1. 2.		1. visible	1.

B. READING

Batter Up

A baseball pitcher's <u>domain</u> is usually limited to an <u>aggregate</u> of three kinds of pitches, such as a fast ball, a curve ball, and a slider. A batter has an <u>incentive</u> to limit his swing to the kind of pitch that he can hit. He, therefore, tries to <u>release</u> his swing only after the rotation of the ball becomes <u>visible</u>.

C. COMPREHENSION CHECK
Exercise 1
Refer to the reading above and use the context to guess the meanings of the words below. Then match the words to their definitions. Do NOT use a dictionary.

___ 1. aggregate   A. something made of separate parts

___ 2. domain   B. to let go of something

___ 3. incentive   C. an area of responsibility or knowledge

___ 4. release   D. able to be seen

___ 5. visible   E. motivation

Exercise 2
Fill in the blanks with the word from the list above that makes sense according to the context.

1. After the Civil War, the Emancipation Proclamation made it mandatory to _____ slaves from forced labor.

2. The _____ to do our research papers early is the 5-point bonus promised by our professor for all papers received the week before they are due.

3. In the _____ of science, there exist things so small they require a powerful microscope to be studied and things so vast they require a powerful telescope to be brought into view.

4. The USA is a/an _____ of people from a multitude of nationalities.

5. In many large cities the air pollution is _____ in the sky from miles away.

6. In order to make the sculptures for their senior projects, the art students gathered gravel and sand to make a/an _____ of cement.

7. After serving a sentence of 10 years for his crime, the prisoner was _____.

8. The cell phone company offered a free phone as a/an _____ to sign up.

9. The King Arthur legends we studied in literature class portray a king with great concern for the people under his _____ .

10. In a word processing class, we learned both how to keep text _____ and how to hide it.

D. WORD STUDY
Exercise
Think of the 5 words in this lesson as causes, and write the effects they might cause to the right below.

1. What are the effects of the U.S. having an <u>aggregate</u> population?	
2. What are the effects of <u>incentive</u> awards for sales people?	
3. What are the effects of a country being under the <u>domain</u> of another country?	
4. What are the effects of signing a <u>release</u> form?	
5. What are the <u>visible</u> effects of staying in the sun for long hours?	

E. USING WORDS IN COMMUNICATION
Exercise
With a partner, discuss the questions below.

1. If for one year, you could be <u>released</u> from all your responsibilities and had no financial constraints, what would you most like to do?

2. In a blizzard, dense fog, rainstorm, sandstorm, or hurricane, <u>visibility</u> can sometimes be reduced to zero. Describe a personal experience you may have had with zero visibility. If you can't think of one, describe one you have seen in a movie or read about in a book.

3. Advertising often uses <u>incentives</u> to attract customers. List three incentives you think would attract college students to buy a product.

4. Before 1776, The USA was under the <u>domain</u> of England. Make a list of other countries that were at one time under England's domain.

LESSON 2

A. WORD FAMILIES

Study the five word families below. Then fill in the word form chart. The underlined word forms at the top of the list are the most commonly used forms in academic texts.

explicit	prohibit	reverse (2X)	transmission	ultimately
/ɪkˈsplɪsɪt/	/prouˈhɪbɪt/	/rəˈvɜrs/	/trænsˈmɪʃən/	/ˈʌltəmɪtli/
explicitly	prohibition	reversal	transmit	ultimate (2X)
	prohibitive	reversible	transmitted	
		irreversible		

Exercise - Word Form Chart

NOUN	VERB	ADJECTIVE	ADVERB
		1. explicit	1.
1.	1. prohibit	1.	
1. 2.	1. reverse	1. 2.	
1. transmission	1.	1.	
1.		1.	1. ultimately

B. READING

Censor the Internet?

Some people believe that public facilities such as libraries and schools should be required by law to use software that blocks and <u>prohibits</u> the <u>transmission</u> of sexually <u>explicit</u> material over the Internet. If this became a law, however, groups that oppose censorship would <u>ultimately</u> go to court to try to <u>reverse</u> such a law.

C. COMPREHENSION CHECK
Exercise 1
Refer to the reading above and use the context to guess the meanings of the words below.
Then match the words to their definitions. Do NOT use a dictionary.

___ 1. explicit	A.	in the end
___ 2. prohibit	B.	forbid, prevent from happening
___ 3. reverse	C.	to go in a backwards direction
___ 4. transmission	D.	giving every detail openly
___ 5. ultimately	E.	passage from one thing to another, the spread of something

Exercise 2
Put YES on the line if the word is used correctly, and NO, if it is not.

___ 1. He <u>ultimately</u> complained immediately after the problem began.

___ 2. The <u>transmission</u> of communicable diseases like tuberculosis still poses a serious health threat in some countries.

___ 3. The grounding of all aircraft because of zero visibility <u>prohibited</u> our departure for our geology field trip to Nevada.

___ 4. The lawyers tried to <u>reverse</u> the decision of the jury by showing that the rights of the prisoner had been violated.

___ 5. Her directions are so <u>explicit</u> I can never understand exactly what she wants.

D. WORD STUDY
Exercise 1
Listed below are three meanings of the word **transmission**.

1. transmission (n) - the assembly that changes gears in an engine
2. transmission (n) - a media broadcast
3. transmission (n) - passage from one thing to another

Decide which meaning of transmission is used in the following sentences. Use 1, 2, or 3 to mark which meaning applies in the sentences.

___ 1. The <u>transmission</u> was interrupted by severe weather.

___ 2. Five-speed <u>transmission</u> cars are a challenge to drive in mountainous terrain.

___ 3. Dentists, nurses, doctors, and ambulance workers wear rubber gloves to prevent the <u>transmission</u> of germs and diseases.

Exercise 2

There are some specific sociological contexts in which three of the words from this lesson are commonly used.

> **Prohibition** refers to a time from 1920-1933 in the United States when the production, transportation, and purchasing of liquor for drinking was forbidden by law.
>
> If you look up the rating of current movies, you may see the information that a movie is rated *R* due to sexually **explicit** content.
>
> Sexually **transmitted** diseases (STDs) are diseases that are spread through sexual contact.

These words are also used for many other situations. In the chart below, write examples of other things that can be prohibited, explicit, and transmitted.

Words	Examples
prohibited	
explicit	
transmitted	

E. USING WORDS IN COMMUNICATION
Exercise

1. Pretend that you bought a car with a bad transmission. With a partner, take turns being the car owner and the automobile dealer. As the car owner, give an <u>explicit</u> complaint about a problem that your car transmission is giving you. Try to use all the words from this lesson. As the automobile dealer, ask questions to get more details about the problem.

2. Practice giving <u>explicit</u> complaints to other merchants or companies you do business with (e.g., banks, credit card companies, phone companies). Try to use the words from this lesson.

3. Role play for the entire class one of the situations from items one or two above.

4. If you could <u>reverse</u> a decision that you have made, what would it be?

5. <u>Ultimately</u>, what do you hope your life will be like?

LESSON 3

A. WORD FAMILIES

Study the five word families below. Then fill in the word form chart. The underlined word forms at the top of the list are the most commonly used forms in academic texts.

comprise	contradiction	interval	publication	subsidiary (2X)
/kəmˈpraɪz/	/ˌkɑntrəˈdɪktʃən/	/ˈɪntərvəl/	/ˌpʌblɪˈkeɪʃən/	/səbˈsɪdiˌɛri/
	contradict			subsidy
				subsidize
				subsidized

Exercise - Word Form Chart

NOUN	VERB	ADJECTIVE	ADVERB
	1. comprise		
1. contradiction	1.		
1. interval			
1. publication			
1. 2.	1.	1. subsidiary 2.	

B. READING

How to Solve a Mystery

In a mystery-type <u>publication</u>, the detective solves a crime by using logic to overcome the <u>contradictions</u> presented by the different characters. Clues are usually presented to the reader at regular <u>intervals</u>. The events surrounding the crime <u>comprise</u> the main plot while humor or romance is often a <u>subsidiary</u> element in the story.

C. COMPREHENSION CHECK
Exercise 1
Refer to the reading above and use the context to guess the meanings of the words below. Then match the words to their definitions. Do NOT use a dictionary.

___ 1. comprise   A. to include, to contain

___ 2. contradiction   B. time periods between events

___ 3. intervals   C. less important, secondary

___ 4. publication   D. something that disagrees with something else

___ 5. subsidiary   E. a book, magazine, or newspaper

Exercise 2
Complete each sentence with the most suitable word. Be sure to change the noun and verb endings if needed.

comprise   contradiction   interval   publication   subsidiary

1. The _____ date of my original edition of *Ben-Hur* is 1880. It is a volume I treasure.

2. The _____ between the assignment of the term paper and the due date seems sufficient until you start working on it.

3. Extra-curricular activities are a big part of college life, but they are _____ to getting an education.

4. The Dallas Independent School District _____ over 300 schools.

5. Criminal justice majors are taught to look for _____ in the stories told them by those they interrogate.

D. WORD STUDY
Exercise 1
Cross out an item (a word or expression) that DOES NOT go with the underlined word. In each list, one or two items may be crossed out.

1. A <u>contradiction</u> exists if   the same story is told but with different times.
you like both hot coffee and iced coffee.
some fact is both true and false.
two people tell the same story but with different details.

2. Many companies <u>comprise</u>   executives, managers, salespersons, and workers.
facilities at more than one location.
morning and evening.

3. There is an <u>interval</u> between

the years of going to elementary school and college.
the introduction of a story and its conclusion.
the author of a book and its publisher.
morning classes and afternoon classes.

Novels
Plays
4. Student speeches
Live concerts
Magazines

can be <u>publications</u>.

Exercise 2

Study the different meanings of the various word forms of the word **subsidiary,** and then do the exercise that follows.

---

1. subsidiary (adj) - less important, secondary
2. subsidiary (n) - a company dependent on another company
3. subsidy (n) - money that is paid to a person, group, or business that is not self-supporting
4. subsidize (v) - to give money to a person, groups, or business to support it or them

---

1. Tide Corporation is a _____ of Proctor and Gamble.

2. Many large corporations _____ university research projects, which makes it possible to pay the graduate students who do the research.

3. The goal for this course is to learn the needed information to pass the Graduate Record Examination (GRE). A _____ goal is to improve your vocabulary, so that reading in graduate courses will be more understandable.

4. The _____ we receive from the university is not enough to live on. We have to supplement it with money from our parents or from our own savings.

E. USING WORDS IN COMMUNICATION
Exercise - Lists

1. List three of your interests that are <u>subsidiary</u> to your main goal of getting an education.

2. List three <u>contradictions</u> between what is important to you and what you do with your time.

3. List three <u>publications</u> you read on a regular basis.

LESSON 4

A. WORD FAMILIES

Study the five word families below. Then fill in the word form chart. The underlined word forms at the top of the list are the most commonly used forms in academic texts.

edition	initiative	survive	topic	voluntary
/əˈdɪʃən/	/ɪˈnɪʃətɪv/	/sərˈvaiv/	/ˈtɑpɪk/	/ˈvɑlənˌtɛri/
edit	initiate	survival	topical	volunteer
editor	initiator	survivor		voluntarily
edited	initiated	surviving		
editing	initiating			
editorial	initiation			

Exercise - Word Form Chart

NOUN	VERB	ADJECTIVE	ADVERB
1. edition 2. 3.	1.	1. 2.	
1. initiative 2. 3.	1.	1. 2.	
1. 2.	1. survive	1.	
1. topic		1.	
1.		1. voluntary	1.

B. READING

Charitable News

Our city newspaper recently published a special section on charitable organizations. One of the articles on the front page of the section was about the <u>voluntary</u> renovation of several houses in the downtown area by ordinary citizens. The <u>topic</u> for another article had been <u>initiatives</u> that Habitat for Humanity had planned for building three houses downtown. However, this article did not <u>survive</u> the cuts for the final <u>edition.</u>

C. COMPREHENSION CHECK
Exercise 1
Refer to the reading above and use the context to guess the meanings of the words below. Then match the words to their definitions. Do NOT use a dictionary.

___ 1. edition
___ 2. initiatives
___ 3. survive
___ 4. topic
___ 5. voluntary

A. plans for the beginning of something
B. to continue to live, to endure
C. a subject of writing or conversation
D. a specific printing of a book or periodical
E. done of one's own will without force or pay

Exercise 2
Circle the word does not belong.

1. survive	last	sustain	quit
2. initiatives	conclusions	proposals	plans
3. duty	charitable	voluntary	unpaid
4. cite	theme	subject	topic
5. version	edition	prohibition	publication

D. WORD STUDY
Exercise
Study the following definitions of the different forms of **initiate**. Then match the sentence halves below.

1. initiative (n) - showing strength or ambition, plan or process started to solve a problem
2. initiate (v) - to cause something to start
3. initiation (n) - to bring someone into an organization
4. initiator (n) - someone who starts something

___ 1. He initiated
___ 2. The initiator of the tax-reform bill that is before Congress
___ 3. The president's peace initiative
___ 4. Initiative is something
___ 5. His initiation into the law firm

A. involved menial cases and working into the late hours of most nights.
B. has not been accepted by the two countries.
C. is very determined to see it put into effect.
D. the discussion of their relationship.
E. that she has in abundance.

E. USING WORDS IN COMMUNICATION
Exercise

With a partner, discuss the questions and statements below.

1. <u>Volunteering</u> at some task implies a love for that task or cause. Is there some area of need in the world that you are passionate enough about that you would offer your time and services as a <u>volunteer</u>? Explain.

2. What is the biggest challenge you have <u>survived</u>?

3. What <u>topic</u> would be painful, or difficult, for you to discuss?

4. Do you prefer to read a morning <u>edition</u> of the newspaper or an afternoon <u>edition</u>? Do you prefer a national <u>edition</u> of the news or a local <u>edition</u>?

REVIEW

Match the clauses on the left with the words on the right to best complete each sentence. On the line at left, write the letter of the word.

___ 1. An area of knowledge or responsibility is a ...	A. aggregate
___ 2. The motivation to do something is its ...	B. comprise
___ 3. If something is easy to see, or obvious, it is...	C. contradiction
___ 4. To let something go is to __ it.	D. domain
___ 5. Something made of separate parts is an...	E. edition
___ 6. A backwards direction is...	F. explicit
___ 7. If drinking is not allowed in your country, it is...	G. incentive
___ 8. A procrastinator starts his assignments late, but he does do them...	H. initiatives
___ 9. Early movies left sexual scenes to the viewer's imagination. Nowadays, things are much more...	I. interval
___ 10. The news of today can be heard around the world within minutes, thanks to radio and television...	J. prohibited
___ 11. A subject of a discussion or a writing is the...	K. publication
___ 12. A smaller company under a larger one is a...	L. release
___ 13. If you don't die in a terrible accident, you...	M. reverse
___ 14. A book, magazine, or newspaper is a...	N. subsidiary
___ 15. To include or contain is to...	O. survive
___ 16. The beginning ideas for something are...	P. topic
___ 17. If you don't get paid to do something and if it is not required, it is...	Q. transmissions
___ 18. If something disagrees with something else, there is a...	R. ultimately
___ 19. A book from its first printing is a first...	S. visible
___ 20. The time period between two events is a time...	T. voluntary

UNIT 6

ACADEMIC WORD POWER

LESSON 1

A. WORD FAMILIES

Study the five word families below. Then fill in the word form chart. The underlined word forms at the top of the list are the most commonly used forms in academic texts.

differentiation	empirical	hierarchical	incidence	incorporate
/ˌdɪfərⱺ̃ntiˈeɪʃən/	/ɛmˈpɪrəkəl/	/ˌhaɪəˈrɑrkɪkəl/	/ˈɪnsədəns/	/ɪnˈkɔrpərˌeɪt/
differentiate	empiricism	hierarchy	incident	incorporation
differentiated	empirically		incidentally	
differentiating				

Exercise - Word Form Chart

NOUN	VERB	ADJECTIVE	ADVERB
1. differentiation	1.	1. 2.	
1.		1. empirical	1.
1.		1. hierarchical	
1. incidence 2.			1.
1.	1. incorporate		

B. READING

The Scientific Method

Research is based on using <u>empirical</u> evidence to answer questions <u>incorporated</u> in a hypothesis. Data may include such things as <u>incidence</u> of occurance, <u>heirarchical</u> ranking of performance, or the presence/absence of certain characteristics. Scientists must take into account the <u>differentiation</u> among test results when forming their conclusions.

C. COMPREHENSION CHECK
Exercise 1
Refer to the reading above and use the context to guess the meanings of the words below. Then match the words to their definitions. Do NOT use a dictionary.

___ 1. differentiation   A. observable, based on knowledge of the real world
___ 2. empirical   B. frequency of something happening
___ 3. hierarchical   C. organized in a higher to lower rank
___ 4. incidence   D. included, contained
___ 5. incorporated   E. the process of finding differences

Exercise 2
Cross out the word that does not belong.

1. discrimination	differentiation	unity	separation
2. observed	experienced	empirical	unclear
3. hierarchical	ranked	randomized	leveled
4. occurrence	frequency	bias	incidence
5. incorporated	included	eliminated	integrated

D. WORD STUDY
Exercise 1
The meaning of the word **incidence** and its other word forms are clarified below:

The words **incidence** and **incidents** sound exactly the same in English pronunciation.

The difference in meaning is:
1. **Incidents** is the plural of the noun incident which means an event, an occurrence.
2. **Incidence** is a singular non-count noun meaning frequency of something happening.

Incidental (adj) means a. minor, or inconsequential,
                            b. secondary to, less important.

Incidentally (adv) is used to introduce a new thought. It means *by the way*.

Read the following sentences and decide which of the forms of **incidence** is needed.

1. The _____ of cheating is increasing on many U.S. campuses.

2. The cost for food was surprisingly low on our study abroad trip to Rome. It was an _____ expense compared to the cost for hotels.

3. _____ , that professor has his doctorate from Cambridge.

4. The short papers required for our psychology course are _____ compared to the final paper.

5. Working in the biology lab required me to count the _____ of caged rats eating from a certain kind of food.

Exercise 2
The meanings of the word **differentiate** are clarified below.

---

1. differentiate (v) - to describe or show differences

2. differentiate (v) - to see or distinguish differences

3. differentiate (v) - to make or develop differences

Choose which meaning is used in the following sentences, and put the number corresponding to it on the line.

___1. Some people who are colorblind cannot <u>differentiate</u> between red and blue.

___2. The computer programmers need to <u>differentiate</u> their product from the other similar products on the market.

___3. When listening to native English speakers, it is difficult for Chinese, Japanese, and Korean speakers to <u>differentiate</u> the English sounds of *l* and *r*.

___4. The business professor spent two class periods <u>differentiating</u> between a partnership and a corporation.

___5. Musicians need to <u>differentiate</u> their playing performance in some way that makes them stand out from other excellent musicians.

E. USING WORDS IN COMMUNICATION
Exercise
Write three sentences using three of the words from this lesson (**differentiation, empirical, hierarchical, incidence** and **incorporated**). In each sentence use one of your classmate's names. You can use any form of the five words.

LESSON 2

A. WORD FAMILIES

Study the five word families below. Then fill in the word form chart. The underlined word forms at the top of the list are the most commonly used forms in academic texts.

definite	disposal	extract (2X)	finite	trace (2X)
/'dɛfənɪt/	/dɪ'spouzəl/	/ɛk'strækt/	/'faɪ,naɪt/	/treɪs/
definitive	dispose	extracted	infinite	traceable
definitely	disposable	extraction	infinitely	
indefinite				
indefinitely				

Exercise - Word Form Chart

NOUN	VERB	ADJECTIVE	ADVERB
		1. definite 2. 3.	1. 2.
1. disposal	1.	1.	
1. 2.	1. extract	1.	
		1. finite 2.	1.
1. trace	1.	1.	

B. READING

Impurities in Water

Water often contains a <u>finite</u> number of impurities, one of which is arsenic. The conclusions from environmental studies have not been <u>definitive</u>, but it is assumed that even a minimal <u>trace</u> of arsenic may be somewhat dangerous to one's health. Therefore, until one can be <u>definite</u> that small amounts of arsenic are harmless, water treatment facilities need to <u>extract</u> the arsenic from the water supplies and arrange for its safe <u>disposal</u>.

C. COMPREHENSION CHECK
Exercise 1
Refer to the reading above and use the context to guess the meanings of the words below. Then match the words to their definitions. Do NOT use a dictionary.

___ 1. definite   A. to remove

___ 2. disposal   B. without doubt, certain

___ 3. extract   C. limited in number

___ 4. finite   D. a very small amount

___ 5. trace   E. the throwing away of

Exercise 2
Fill in the blanks with the correct word from the list above.

1. There was not even a _____ of evidence against the thief, so he was not convicted.
2. The dentist had to put her to sleep to _____ her wisdom teeth.
3. The _____ of needles and other medical supplies that come in contact with blood has to be done very carefully as a precaution against the spread of HIV and other diseases spread by contact with blood.
4. There is a _____ correlation between motivation and success.
5. We all have only a _____ number of hours in a day, but some people accomplish so much more in those hours than others do.

D. WORD STUDY
Exercise 1
Consider the multiple meanings for the **trace** and **extract**.

1. trace (n) - a very small amount
2. trace (n) - a hint of evidence, a faint track
3. trace (v) - to follow something to its beginning point
4. trace (v) - to copy onto thin paper from an image underneath

5. extract (v) - to get by using force
6. extract (n) - an essence or concentration of food or some other substance
7. extract (n) - an excerpt from a written work

Decide which word belongs in each sentence at the top of the next page. On the line in front of the sentence, write the number corresponding to the meaning of the word. Change the word form if needed.

____ 1. The hunter used the _____ of footprints to follow the deer.

____ 2. There is a huge market for _____ from flowers, herbs, and spices for the scented candle and perfume businesses.

____ 3. The student teachers tried to _____ the pictures with their elementary school students.

____ 4. Police sometimes use force to _____ information from a prisoner.

____ 5. In chemistry lab, the students had to detect even a _____ of any dangerous elements.

____ 6. The FBI attempts to _____ the path of computer viruses that shut down computer networks around the world.

____ 7. The tabloid writer _____ an incidental point from the politician's speech and made it the only issue.

Exercise 2
Consider the idiomatic use of the word **disposal**.

Many students came to help their classmate who had broken her leg. They all wanted to help and kept saying, "We are **at your disposal**."

What does it mean to be at someone's disposal?

_____

_____

_____

E. USING WORDS IN COMMUNICATION
Exercise
With a partner, in five minutes, write down as many examples of the five words from this unit as you can.

	Examples:
Things that are definite:	
Things you extract:	
Finite things:	
Things that are disposable:	
Things used to trace a criminal:	

LESSON 3

A. WORD FAMILIES

Study the five word families below. Then fill in the word form chart. The underlined word forms at the top of the list are the most commonly used forms in academic texts.

allocation clarity revision scope (2X) submit
/ˌæləˈkeɪʃən/ /ˈklærəti/ /rəˈvɪʒən/ /skoup/ /səbˈmɪt/
allocate clarify revise   submitted
allocated clarified revised   submission
 clarifying revising
 clarification

Exercise - Word Form Chart

NOUN	VERB	ADJECTIVE	ADVERB
1. allocation	1.	1.	
1. clarity 2.	1.	1. 2.	
1. revision	1.	1. 2.	
1. scope	1.		
1.	1. submit	1.	

B. READING

The City Budget

The city manager <u>submitted</u> his report for the <u>allocation</u> of funds for next year's budget. The <u>scope</u> of the budget included everything from the mayor's salary to the gas needed for the garbage trucks. The city council requested a <u>revision</u> to give <u>clarity</u> to one confusing part of the budget. Other than that, it was all accepted.

C. COMPREHENSION CHECK
Exercise 1
Refer to the reading above and use the context to guess the meanings of the words below. Then match the words to their definitions. Do NOT use a dictionary.

___ 1. allocation		A.	clearness of ideas in writing or speaking
___ 2. clarity		B.	the limits or range of something
___ 3. revision		C.	the plan to use an amount of time, money, or other resources for a specific purpose
___ 4. scope		D.	the process of editing something
___ 5. submitted		E.	passed in or given to someone

Exercise 2
Write YES if the statement using a word from this lesson makes sense, and NO if it does not.

_____ 1. The <u>allocation</u> of the old library building for future apartments would solve the housing problem.

_____ 2. The paper received a low grade because of its <u>clarity</u>.

_____ 3. The <u>revision</u> of his work never takes long since he writes so carefully as he works.

_____ 4. Since the topic for our composition was to compare public transportation in our university city to that of our hometown, the <u>scope</u> needed to include the cost of hotel rooms.

_____ 5. Robert <u>submitted</u> from exhaustion and spent two days in the hospital.

D. WORD STUDY
Exercise
Study the multiple meanings of the verb **submit**, and then do the exercise that follows.

1. submit (v) - to agree, to comply
2. submit (v) - to pass in or give something to someone
3. submit (v) - to introduce or propose something

Match the clauses on the left with those on the right to best complete each sentence. On the line at left, write the number corresponding to the meaning of submit. (1, 2, 3)

___ 1.	The students had to submit	A.	a proposal for a tax-reform model.
___ 2.	Child psychologists tell us that strong willed children have a hard time submitting	B.	their papers two weeks before the end of the semester.
___ 3.	A retired accountant and business professor submitted	D.	to their parents' guidelines unless they are strictly enforced.

E. USING WORDS IN COMMUNICATION
Exercise

You and your partner are on the budget committee for a campus charity organization that has raised or collected $10,000. It is your job to make a proposal on how much money to <u>allocate</u> for each of the approved projects. You are then to <u>submit</u> a report <u>clarifying</u> why you chose the <u>allocations</u> that you did.

Amount	Project
_____	1. 10 new beds and linens for the homeless shelter
_____	2. the gymnasium building project at the orphanage
_____	3. Habitat for Humanity, for 5 proposed houses to be built for low-income people this year
_____	4. refugee relief for newly arrived refugees

Report for Clarification:

LESSON 4

A. WORD FAMILIES
Study the five word families below. Then fill in the word form chart. The underlined word forms at the top of the list are the most commonly used forms in academic texts.

adaptation	convert (2X)	inhibition	prospect	termination
/ˌædəpˈteɪʃən/	/kənˈvɜrt/	/ˌɪnhəˈbɪʃən/	/ˈprɑsˌpɛkt/	/ˌtɜrməˈneɪʃən/
adapt	converted	inhibit	prospective	terminal (2X)
adapted	conversion	inhibited		terminate
adaptive	convertible	inhibiting		terminated
adaptable				terminating
adaptability				

Exercise - Word Form Chart

NOUN	VERB	ADJECTIVE	ADVERB
1. adaptation 2.	1.	1. 2. 3.	
1. 2.	1. convert	1. 2.	
1. inhibition	1.	1. 2.	
1. prospect		1.	
1. termination 2.	1.	1. 2. 3.	

B. READING

Job Search

After his <u>termination</u> from his former company, the <u>prospect</u> of looking for a new job frightened Jake. However, through the skills he learned at a job search workshop, his fear was <u>converted</u> to enthusiasm for the new possibilities he could have. An <u>adaptation</u> of his resume to meet the expectations of employers in a new, technical, and computerized job market was necessary. After attending the workshop, his earlier <u>inhibition</u> about the job search was gone.

C. COMPREHENSION CHECK
Exercise 1
Refer to the reading above and use the context to guess the meanings of the words below. Then match the words to their definitions. Do NOT use a dictionary.

____ 1. adaptation

____ 2. converted

____ 3. inhibition

____ 4. prospect

____ 5. termination

A. the firing from employment

B. something psychological that makes a certain behavior difficult

C. anticipation of a future event

D. adjustments needed to function in a new way

E. changed the condition of something

Exercise 2
Write YES if the underlined word is used correctly and NO if it is not.

____ 1. Her strong social inhibitions allow her to be friendly with everyone.

____ 2. He converted his money to dollars upon his arrival in the United States.

____ 3. No one fears job termination in a time of recession.

____ 4. The popular novel's adaptation to a new format was disappointing. Most fans agreed that too many changes were made to characters and plot in the new TV version.

____ 5. The prospect of moving to another country is both exciting and frightening.

D. WORD STUDY
Exercise
Consider the multiple meanings for **termination** and its word forms:

1. terminate (v) - to end, to stop

2. terminate (v) - to fire from employment

3. terminal (n) - a station or depot (train, bus, airline)

4. terminal (n) - the last stop on a means of transportation

5. terminal (n) - an electrical post

6. terminal (n) - a machine that works by being connected to another computer and that does not have a CPU (central processing unit) of its own.

7. terminal (adj) - fatal, or causing death

Choose which answer best completes each sentence on the next page.

Choose which answer best completes each sentence

1. If your roommate is at the <u>terminal</u>,
   a. she is ill.
   b. she may need a ride back to campus.
   c. she is working at a computer that is connected to a CPU.

2. If your grandfather is at the hospital and the doctor told him that his disease is <u>terminal</u>,
   a. surgery will take care of his problem.
   b. he will be taking strong drugs to cure his illness.
   c. you should make plans to see him as soon as possible.

3. If your father received a <u>termination</u> notice at work,
   a. he was transferred to another city.
   b. he completed his project.
   c. he was fired.

E. USING WORDS IN COMMUNICATION
Exercise
With a partner, discuss the following questions.

1. Would you describe yourself as <u>inhibited</u>? In what situations do you feel the most <u>inhibition</u>?

2. Have you, or has another family member, been <u>terminated</u> from a job? What helped you, or them, get another job?

3. What should you do to impress a <u>prospective</u> employer in an interview?

4. Studying in another country requires an incredible <u>adaptability</u>. What other qualities could help you live successfully in a foreign country?

5. Give an example of a <u>conversion</u> you've witnessed? (e.g., personalities, religion, life-style, buildings, goals, etc.)

REVIEW

Circle words and draw lines between words you associate with each other. There is not one correct word association, and you may have more than one with certain words and no associations with other words. Think about why you make these associations and be able to explain to a partner.

adaptations   empirical

definite   hierarchical

disposal   converted

finite   empirical

differentiation   clarity

submitted   prospect

trace   inhibition

extracted   allocation

termination   incidence

incorporated   hierarchical

revision   scope

UNIT 7

WORDS

abandon	exhibit	manipulation	thereby
accompany	fluctuation	predominantly	uniform
assign	ideology	radical	vehicle
detect	insert	reinforce	via
dramatic	intensity	theme	virtually

READINGS

Teenage Rebellion
The Media: A Tool for Hate
A Bright Fire
An Engineering Experiment

STRATEGIES AND SKILLS

Word Forms
- Word family chart
- Word form selection

Comprehension Check
- Matching definitions
- Understanding and using words in context
- Identifying synonyms
- Pairing sentence halves
- Identifying antonyms

Word Expansion
- Multiple meanings
- Categorizing
- Collocations

Interactive Speaking Practice
- Sentence completion
- Summarizing
- Discussion

ACADEMIC WORD POWER

LESSON 1

A. WORD FAMILIES

Study the five word families below. Then fill in the word form chart. The underlined word forms at the top of the list are the most commonly used forms in academic texts.

abandon	dramatic	ideology	radical (2X)	predominantly
/əˈbændən/	/drəˈmætik/	/ˌaɪdiˈɑlədʒi/	/ˈrædəkəl/	/prɪˈdɑməˌnəntli/
abandoned	drama		radically	predominate
abandonment	dramatist			predominant
	dramatize			predominating
	dramatization			predominance
	dramatically			

Exercise - Word Form Chart

NOUN	VERB	ADJECTIVE	ADVERB
1.	1. abandon	1.	
1. 2. 3.	1.	1. dramatic	1.
1. ideology			
1.		1. radical	1.
1.	1.	1. 2.	1. predominantly

B. READING

Teenage Rebellion

As adolescents in the United States come of age, a <u>dramatic</u>, although common, form of rebellion occurs in their political thinking. Children often <u>abandon</u> their parents' moderate <u>ideology</u> in favor of more <u>radical</u> ways of thinking. This period of rebellion is usually relatively short, however, and takes place <u>predominantly</u> in the late teens and early twenties. With middle age, most people return to a moderate stance.

C. COMPREHENSION CHECK
Exercise 1
Refer to the reading above and use the context to guess the meanings of the words below. Then match the words to their definitions. Do NOT use a dictionary.

___ 1. abandon   A. primarily, mostly
___ 2. dramatic   B. a set of beliefs
___ 3. ideology   C. striking, forceful
___ 4. predominantly   D. non-traditional, extreme change
___ 5. radical   E. to leave

Exercise 2
True or False? Write T or F in the blanks provided.

___ 1. If you live at home and work in your father's company, you abandon your family's traditions.

___ 2. In the 1960s, a radical way of dressing was with flowers in the hair, bell-bottom jeans, no shoes, and no makeup. Today one radical way of dressing is covering the body with tattoos, piercing various body parts, and dying the hair bright colors.

___ 3. If something is true most of the time, it is predominantly true.

___ 4. People with a strong ideology don't know what they believe.

___ 5. If a student changes his major from chemistry to bio-chemistry, he is making a dramatic change.

Exercise 3
Cross out the word that does not belong.

1. abandon	keep	desert	leave
2. dramatic	shy	strong	forceful
3. ideology	beliefs	doubts	opinions
4. predominantly	occasionally	primarily	usually
5. radical	moderate	extreme	excessive

D. WORD STUDY
Exercise 1
Consider these different meanings of the word **radical**.

1. radical (n) - one who holds or follows extreme principles, an extremist in politics
2. radical (n) - (in math) a quantity expressed as a root of another quantity
3. radical (n) - (in chemistry) an atom that is an important constituent of the molecule of a given compound
4. radical (adj) - very unusual, different from what is normal
5. radical (adj) - going to the center or source of something
6. radically (adv) - completely

At the top of the next page, write four sentences using four different meanings of **radical**.

1. _____

2. _____

3. _____

4. _____

Exercise 2

Study the multiple meanings and uses of the following words from this lesson, and then do the exercise that follows.

---

1. **predominantly (adv)** - mostly, primarily
   Note: This word often appears in the context of describing the population of a neighborhood, a school, or other area or institution. (i.e. predominantly white, predominantly middle-class, predominantly Hispanic, predominantly rich, predominantly poor, etc.)
2. **predominant (adj)** - superior in strength, having authority over others
3. **predominant (adj)** - most frequent or noticeable
4. **predominate (v)** - overshadow others

---

5. **drama (n)** - a play, film, or book (usually a serious one)
6. **dramatic (adj)** - forceful, striking
7. **dramatic (adj)** - having the characteristics of a drama
8. **dramatize (v)** - to act in an exaggerated way, as though in a play
9. **dramatist (n)** - a playwright, one who writes plays

---

10. **abandon (v)** - to leave, to renounce, to give up
11. **abandonment (n)** - freedom from conventional restraint, wildness, recklessness

---

Write YES is the word is used correctly and NO if it is not.

_____ 1. The Mardi Gras celebration in New Orleans is a time of complete <u>abandonment</u> for many of those who attend. People dance in the streets and party all night.

_____ 2. The game of chess is <u>predominantly</u> a physical skill.

_____ 3. Kathryn is so <u>dramatic</u>. She tells stories in a boring, uninteresting manner.

_____ 4. For Asians, a <u>predominant</u> physical feature of Americans is their large noses. As a matter of fact, in the past Americans were called "those with big noses."

_____ 5. Shakespeare was a famous <u>dramatist</u>, and his plays are still acted today.

_____ 6. Women who <u>abandon</u> their families stay in a marriage no matter how difficult it may be.

_____ 7. Picasso's painting Guernica is a famous <u>drama</u>.

_____ 8. Professor Clark <u>dramatizes</u> his lecture about violence by firing a gun loaded with blanks in class.

E. USING WORDS IN COMMUNICATION
Exercise

With a partner, complete these sentences.

1. My childhood neighborhood was <u>predominantly</u>…

2. There are many <u>abandoned</u> animals…

3. A <u>radical</u> thing to do would be to…

4. A common <u>ideology</u> among my friends is…

5. A very <u>dramatic</u> person I know is _____ , and he/she acts like this:

LESSON 2

A. WORD FAMILIES
Study the five word families below. Then fill in the word form chart. The underlined word forms at the top of the list are the most commonly used forms in academic texts.

<u>detect</u>	<u>manipulation</u>	<u>theme</u>	<u>vehicle</u>	<u>via</u>
/dɪˈtɛkt/	/məˌnɪpyəˈleɪʃən/	/θim/	/ˈviːkəl/	/ˈviə/
detector	manipulate	thematic		
detective	manipulating	thematically		
detection	manipulative			
detectable				

Exercise - Word Form Chart

NOUN	VERB	ADJECTIVE	ADVERB	PREPOSITION
1. 2. 3.	1. detect	1.		
1. manipulation	1.	1. 2.		
1. theme		1.	1.	
1. vehicle				
				1. via

B. READING

The Media: A Tool for Hate

Most people believe that part of the media's duty is to report on the views and activities of extremists. However, some argue that media coverage provides a free <u>vehicle</u> for racists to spread their hateful message <u>via</u> the airwaves. Experts have in fact <u>detected</u> a viable basis for concern. Many hate groups teach <u>manipulation</u> of the media by attracting attention to themselves as a way to get new recruits. This issue forms the foundation for a common <u>theme</u> of modern debate: Where does media detachment end and responsibility begin?

C. COMPREHENSION CHECK
Exercise 1

Refer to the reading above and use the context to guess the meanings of the words below.
Then match the words to their definitions. Do NOT use a dictionary.

___ 1. detected   A. observed, noticed
___ 2. manipulation   B. by the way of
___ 3. theme   C. a central idea
___ 4. vehicle   D. devious management, influence for one's personal gain
___ 5. via   E. an instrument of transmission

Exercise 2

Draw lines to match the clauses on the left with those that complete them on the right.

1. The <u>theme</u> of this novel is   A. is <u>via</u> the TGV bullet train.
2. After hearing a loud noise,   B. is e-mail.
3. A primary <u>vehicle</u> for communication between university students and their families   C. <u>manipulation</u> and confront their clients who use it to control people.
4. Psychologists are quick to notice   D. the struggle between social classes.
5. A fast way to travel in France   E. I <u>detected</u> a problem in the way my car was operating.

D. WORD STUDY
Exercise 1

Consider the various meanings of the word **manipulation**:

1. manipulation -	working or operating with the hands	
2. manipulation -	influencing someone/something shrewdly for one's own advantage	
3. manipulation -	changing or falsifying something (figures, accounts, etc.) to one's own advantage	

Complete the following sentences which use the various forms of manipulation.

1. His skillful <u>manipulation</u> of the landing controls on the airplane...

2. Through computer programs, photographs can be <u>manipulated</u> to

3. His use of anger to <u>manipulate</u> his wife...

Here are some possible answers to the Word Study above. How do your answers compare?

1. ...saved our lives when he had to land the plane in a storm.
2. ...look like they occurred at any location, in any kind of weather.
3. ...was obvious to everyone except to her.

Exercise 2

The usual meaning of **vehicle** is a means of human transportation, such as cars, buses, trains, etc. The meaning used in the reading for this lesson is also a means of transportation, but the object being transported is an idea.

Make a list of different kinds of vehicles under the two headings below.

Vehicles for human transportation	Vehicles for ideas

E. USING WORDS IN COMMUNICATION

Exercise

With a partner, discuss the following.

1. Review the reading for this lesson. Then, without looking, tell your partner the information from the paragraph. Discuss together the two views about the media presented in this paragraph.

2. What have you <u>detected</u> about your roommate or friend?

3. What is a <u>theme</u> of modern debate in the world?

4. What <u>vehicle</u> of communication (e-mail, telephone, letters) do you prefer to use?

5. Do you know someone who is <u>manipulative</u>? If so, describe that person.

LESSON 3

A. WORD FAMILIES

Study the five word families below. Then fill in the word form chart. The underlined word forms at the top of the list are the most commonly used forms in academic texts.

exhibit (2X)	intensity	fluctuation	uniform (2X)	virtually
/ɪgˈzɪbɪt/	/ɪnˈtɛnsəti/	/ˈflʌktʃuˌeɪʃən/	/ˈyunəˌfɔrm/	/ˈvɜrtʃuəli/
exhibition	intense	fluctuate	uniformly	virtual
	intensify	fluctuated	uniformity	
	intensive	fluctuating		
	intensely			
	intenseness			
	intensification			

Exercise - Word Form Chart

NOUN	VERB	ADJECTIVE	ADVERB
1. 2.	1. exhibit		
1. intensity 2. 3.	1.	1. 2.	1.
1. fluctuation	1.	1. 2.	
1. 2.		1. uniform	1.
		1.	1. virtually

B. READING

A Bright Fire

When stretched into a thin ribbon and exposed to strong heat, pure magnesium burns with a flame of remarkable intensity. Also remarkable is the fact that magnesium fires exhibit an unusually uniform glow, with very few fluctuations in brightness. The glow is so bright, in fact, that it is virtually unwatchable.

C. COMPREHENSION CHECK
Exercise 1
Refer to the reading above and use the context to guess the meanings of the words below. Then match the words to their definitions. Do NOT use a dictionary.

___ 1. exhibit
___ 2. fluctuations
___ 3. intensity
___ 4. uniform
___ 5. virtually

A. the same all through something
B. nearly, but not quite
C. show, display
D. rising and falling changes
E. the strength of something

Exercise 2
Fill in the blanks with the correct word from the list above.

1. Texas is known for its _____ in temperature. Except for the summer season, temperatures can vary dramatically from one day to the next.

2. The Omaha Beach cemetery at Normandy consists of _____ rows of perfectly aligned crosses and stars marking graves of U.S. soldiers.

3. Away from the haze of city lights, the night sky is_____ black.

4. Mother Teresa's "Sisters of Charity" _____ compassion by caring for the poorest of the poor.

5. The _____ of the sun is greater at the equator than at the North Pole and South Pole.

D. WORD STUDY
Exercise
Study the meanings of the words in this lesson, and then do the exercise that follows.

> 1. intense (adj) - strong in feelings or emotions, concentrated, bright
> 2. intensify (v) - to make something stronger, to increase
> 3. intensity (n) - the degree or strength of something
> 4. intensive (adj) - a lot in a short time

> 5. virtual (adj) - almost, but not quite
> (Note: a contemporary collocation with virtual is virtual reality, meaning an experience that seems real, but is computer generated.)
> 6. uniform (n) - a special type of clothes worn by members of a certain group
> 7. exhibit (n) - a display of something

As quickly as possible, write down things that can be associated with the words below.

1. Things that can be <u>intense</u>:	
2. Things that can be <u>intensive</u>:	
3. <u>Virtual reality</u> things:	
4. Kinds of <u>uniforms:</u>	
5. Kinds of <u>exhibits</u>:	
6. Things that <u>fluctuate</u>:	

E. USING WORDS IN COMMUNICATION
Exercise
Discuss the following with a partner or in a group.

1. Compare your charts for the word study lesson above. Do you have any of the same associations? Explain your associations to your partner.

2. In this lesson, you read that the nuns in Mother Teresa's order <u>exhibit</u> compassion. What traits do you wish you could <u>exhibit</u>?

3. Have you ever had to wear a <u>uniform</u>? If yes, describe it to your partner.

4. Have you ever studied in an <u>intensive</u> program? What made it <u>intensive</u>?

5. Emotions, or feelings, fluctuate rather than stay <u>uniform</u>. Give an example of when your feelings <u>fluctuated</u>.

Lesson 4

A. WORD FAMILIES
Study the five word families below. Then fill in the word form chart. The underlined word forms at the top of the list are the most commonly used forms in academic texts.

accompany	assign	insert (2X)	reinforce	thereby
/əˈkʌmpəni/	/əˈsaɪn/	/ɪnˈsɜrt/	/ˌriɪnˈfɔrs/	/ˈðɛrˌbaɪ/
accompanying	assigned	insertion	reinforced	
accompaniment	reassign	inserted	reinforcement	
	reassigned			
	unassigned			
	assignment			

Exercise - Word Form Chart

NOUN	VERB	ADJECTIVE	ADVERB
1.	1. accompany	1.	
1.	1. assign 2.	1. assigned 2. 3.	
1. 2.	1. insert	1.	
1.	1. reinforced	1.	
			1. thereby

B. READING

An Engineering Experiment

The mechanical engineering teacher gave the following instructions to her students: First, head to your <u>assigned</u> station. You should find two hollow aluminum tubes and a plastic cylinder, <u>accompanied</u> by a vise grip. Take the first aluminum tube, place it in the vise grip, and pull towards you. It will bend easily. Next, <u>insert</u> the plastic cylinder into the second aluminum tube. Place the <u>reinforced</u> tube in the vise grip and pull. The plastic tube will act as a shock absorber, <u>thereby</u> enhancing the tube's horizontal strength.

C. COMPREHENSION CHECK
Exercise 1
Refer to the reading above and use the context to guess the meanings of the words below.
Then match the words to their definitions. Do NOT use a dictionary.

___ 1. accompanied	A. to put something inside something else
___ 2. assigned	B. designated
___ 3. insert	C. in consequence
___ 4. reinforced	D. associated with or connected to
___ 5. thereby	E. made stronger

Exercise 2
Circle the **antonym** of the words from this lesson.

1.	accompany	:	company	alone	associate
2.	assigned	:	listed	appointed	volunteered
3.	insert	:	remove	certain	interject
4.	reinforced	:	forced	weakened	strengthened

D. WORD STUDY
Exercise
Cross out the collocations (combination words) that do not fit with the phrases below.
(1 each)

1. She <u>accompanied</u>
   - her son to the dance.
   - the class on the trip.
   - the bus schedule.
   - the singer on the piano.

2. They were <u>assigned</u>
   - a lot of homework.
   - the early morning class.
   - a specific practice room.
   - impatient.

3. The security measures at the airports
   The fences around the military compound   were <u>reinforced</u>.
   The horses in the field.
   The doors on jet planes

4. He <u>inserted</u>
   - the key into the ignition.
   - the needle into the muscle.
   - a book on top of the stack of books.
   - a paragraph into the letter.

5. Her parents pay her tuition, <u>thereby</u>
   - allowing her to study full time.
   - she can't study.
   - making it easy for her to stay at school.

E. USING WORDS IN COMMUNICATION
Exercise

With a partner, discuss the following questions.

1. Who usually <u>accompanies</u> you to lunch?

2. What airline seat do you like to be <u>assigned</u>?

3. In the United States, there are many advertising <u>inserts</u> in newspapers. What kind of <u>inserts</u> do you find in the newspaper?

4. Describe how you would <u>reinforce</u> a broken backpack strap.

5. What challenges have you faced in life that have <u>thereby</u> made you a stronger person?

ACADEMIC WORD POWER 3

REVIEW

Rearrange these words to form sentences that make sense using the words from this unit. Hint: The first word of the sentence is capitalized, and the commas and periods follow the words that they follow in the sentence

1. at private / are <u>predominantly</u> required / schools. / <u>Uniforms</u>

   _____

2. <u>detected</u>. / is easily / of their relationship / The <u>intensity</u>

   _____

3. France and Italy. / to / We traveled / <u>vehicle</u> / <u>via</u> a / rented

   _____

4. had a war <u>theme</u>, / every painting / The art <u>exhibit</u> / the horrors of war. / so <u>virtually</u> / was about

   _____

   _____

5. many vocal majors / more hours of piano practice / and <u>thereby</u> gained / Paulo <u>accompanied</u> / for himself.

   _____

   _____

6. prior to entering / His low TOEFL score / to be <u>assigned</u> to / a university. / <u>reinforced</u> his need / English classes

   _____

   _____

7. <u>abandoning</u> your / are <u>dramatic</u>. / family / The consequences of

   _____

8. many U.S. citizens thought / In the 1950s, / was a <u>radical</u> / Communism / <u>ideology</u>.

   _____

9. feelings / <u>fluctuations</u> in / <u>Manipulation</u> can cause / toward the manipulator. / people's

   _____

10. his <u>ideology</u> / <u>insert</u> / into / his lectures. / The professor / to / tried not

   _____

104

APPENDICES

A. ACADEMIC WORD LIST INDEX
B. ROOTS, PREFIXES, SUFFIXES

Appendix A
Word List Index

Academic Word List Index

The 140 target words studied in this book come from the Academic Word List (see Introduction, page ix for a description of the AWL). The four volumes of Academic Word Power cover 560 of the 570 words on the AWL. Below is a complete, alphabetical list of the AWL. The numbers indicate the volume, unit and page number where the word is introduced.

Word	v.u.pg	Word	v.u.pg	Word	v.u.pg
abandon	3.7.90	aspect	1.5.65	coincide	4.4.51
abstract	3.3.40	assemble	4.2.18	collapse	4.6.78
academy	2.2.18	assess	1.6.85	colleague	4.1.2
access	2.7.92	assign	3.7.101	commence	4.5.64
accommodate	4.5.70	assist	1.1.8	comment	3.7.96
accompany	3.7.101	assume	3.1.5	commission	1.6.76
accumulate	4.1.8	assure	4.6.78	commitment	2.5.75
accurate	2.7.94	attach	2.6.89	commodity	4.6.81
achieve	1.2.18	attain	4.2.24	communicate	
acknowledge	3.4.46	attitude	2.2.21	community	1.1.2
acquire	1.7.100	attribute	3.1.5	compatible	4.5.60
adapt	3.6.84	author	2.5.75	compensate	2.2.24
adequate	2.6.89	authority	1.4.46	compile	4.5.64
adjacent	4.4.46	automate	3.3.32	complement	4.7.96
adjust	2.5.66	available	1.1.8	complex	1.4.53
administrate	1.4.46	aware	2.4.56	component	4.1.11
adult	3.2.24	behalf	4.5.70	compound	4.3.35
advocate	3.4.46	benefit	1.1.8	comprehensive	3.4.49
affect	1.2.18	bias	3.3.34	comprise	3.5.66
aggregate	3.5.60	bond	4.1.2	compute	1.4.56
aid	3.2.24	brief	2.5.69	conceive	4.7.90
albeit	4.7.99	bulk	4.3.32	concentrate	2.7.94
allocate	3.6.81	capable	3.2.18	concept	1.3.41
alter	2.1.8	capacity	2.6.86	conclude	1.1.11
alternative	2.3.37	category	1.5.71	concurrent	4.7.90
ambiguous	3.4.52	cease	4.4.46	conduct	1.7.90
amend	3.1.8	challenge	2.1.5	confer	4.1.11
analogy	4.4.48	channel	4.1.8	confine	4.6.76
analyze	1.5.68	chapter	1.2.18	confirm	3.3.32
annual	2.1.11	chart	4.3.40	conflict	3.1.2
anticipate	4.1.11	chemical	4.2.18	conform	3.4.52
apparent	2.4.60	circumstance	2.2.21	consent	2.7.100
append	4.3.32	cite	3.4.46	consequent	1.7.93
appreciate	3.2.24	civil	2.5.69	considerable	2.4.50
approach	1.2.18	clarify	3.6.81	consist	1.4.46
appropriate	1.3.32	classic	4.3.32	constitute	
approximate	2.2.28	clause	2.4.60	constant	2.3.43
arbitrary	4.3.38	code	4.2.21	contract	1.5.71
area	1.1.11	coherent	4.6.76	constrain	3.1.8

109

Word	v.u.pg	Word	v.u.pg	Word	v.u.pg
constrain	1.6	differentiate	3.6.74	evaluate	1.2.21
consult	2.6.86	dimension	2.6.86	eventual	3.4.52
consume	1.3.32	diminish	4.3.35	evident	1.3.38
contact	4.3.32	discrete	2.7.100	evolve	2.4.57
contemporary	3.3.34	discriminate	3.4.52	exceed	3.3.32
context	1.218	displace	4.5.70	exclude	1.7.90
contradict	3.5.66	display	2.5.75	exhibit	3.7.97
contrary	4.2.21	dispose	3.6.77	expand	4.3.40
contrast	2.2.24	distinct	1.4.50	expert	2.6.83
contribute	2.3.40	distort	4.7.93	explicit	3.5.63
controversy	4.7.93	distribute	1.5.68	exploit	4.6.76
convene	2.5.75	diverse	3.3.34	export	1.5.71
converse	4.1.2	document	1.7.93	external	2.3.46
convert	3.6.84	domain	3.5.60	extract	3.6.77
convince	4.4.46	domestic	2.4.53	facilitate	4.3.32
cooperate	3.2.27	dominate	2.3.37	factor	1.1.2
coordinate	2.2.94	draft	2.6.86	feature	1.4.50
core	1.7.100	drama	3.7.90	federal	4.2.27
corporate	4.2.24	duration	4.2.27	fee	2.5.66
correspond	2.3.43	dynamic	3.4.55	file	4.1.5
couple		economy	1.4.50	final	1.1.14
create	1.2.21	edit	3.5.69	finance	1.5.62
credit	1.3.32	element	1.3.41	finite	3.6.77
criteria	2.7.104	eliminate	3.2.21	flexible	2.5.75
crucial	3.4.49	emerge	2.3.34	fluctuate	3.7.97
culture	1.1.2	emphasis	1.2.21	focus	1.3.32
currency	4.4.54	empirical	3.6.74	format	4.4.51
cycle	2.2.21	enable	4.1.5	formula	1.7.100
data	1.3.35	encounter	4.3.40	forthcoming	4.5.84
debate	2.2.18	energy	2.1.2	foundation	3.3.37
decade	3.2.21	enforce	3.1.2	found	4.3.40
decline	2.4.50	enhance	3.3.34	framework	2.2.28
deduce	2.2.28	enormous	4.4.54	function	1.5.68
define	1.1.11	ensure	2.1.5	fund	1.7.93
definite	3.6.77	entity	4.2.18	fundamental	2.3.37
demonstrate	2.1.5	environment	1.1.5	furthermore	2.6.89
denote	4.2.27	equate	1.6.82	gender	3.2.18
deny	3.2.18	equip	3.2.21	generate	3.1.11
depress	4.6.76	equivalent	2.5.72	generation	2.2.28
derived	3.1.5	erode	4.4.46	globe	3.3.34
design	1.3.35	error	2.2.24	goal	2.1.8
despite	2.1.8	establish	1.6.79	grade	4.2.21
detect	3.7.94	estate		grant	2.4.57
deviate	4.4.51	estimate	1.5.62	guarantee	3.2.18
device	4.5.64	ethic	4.3.40	guideline	3.3.32
devoted	4.6.78	ethnic	2.4.53	hence	4.1.8

Word	v.u.pg	Word	v.u.pg	Word	v.u.pg
hierarchy	3.6.74	internal	2.2.24	minimum	2.5.69
highlight	3.2.27	interpret	1.4.56	ministry	4.1.2
hypothesis	2.5.72	interval	3.5.66	minor	1.1.5
identical	3.2.24	intervene	3.4.46	mode	3.4.55
ideology	3.7.90	intrinsic	4.6.81	modify	2.3.43
ignorance	2.6.83	invest	1.7.93	monitor	2.6.80
illustrate	2.1.11	investigate	2.3.43	motive	3.1.2
image	2.3.37	invoke	4.6.81	mutual	4.7.90
immigrate	2.2.21	involve	1.2.24	negate	1.6.79
impact	1.5.62	isolate	3.1.8	network	2.4.53
implement	2.7.97	issue	1.7.100	neutral	3.3.40
implicate	4.2.27	item	1.4.50	nevertheless	3.1.5
implicit	4.7.90	job	2.1.8	nonetheless	4.4.54
imply	2.1.11	journal	1.6.79	norm	4.4.51
impose	2.7.104	justify	2.6.83	normal	1.1.5
incentives	3.5.60	label	2.1.2	notion	2.5.72
incidence	3.6.74	labor	1.6.85	notwithstanding	4.7.90
incline	4.7.99	layer	1.7.96	nuclear	4.6.78
income	1.6.76	lecture	2.5.72	objective	2.4.60
incorporate	3.6.74	legal	1.453	obtain	1.5.68
index	4.1.5	legislate	1.5.65	obvious	2.2.24
indicate	1.4.46	levy	4.5.64	occupy	2.2.18
individual	1.2.21	liberal	2.5.66	occur	1.1.5
induce	4.5.60	license	2.3.40	odd	4.5.60
inevitable	4.5.70	likewise	4.2.18	offset	4.7.96
infer	3.2.24	link	1.7.96	ongoing	4.3.38
infrastructure	4.6.78	locate	1.6.82	option	2.3.46
inherent	4.4.48	logic	2.4.57	orient	2.5.66
inhibit	3.6.84	maintain	1.3.38	outcome	2.1.5
initial	1.7.90	major	1.2.24	output	
initiate	3.5.69	manipulate	3.7.94	overall	2.4.57
innovate	3.3.37	manual	4.4.46	overlap	4.4.54
input		margin	2.7.104	overseas	4.1.2
insert	3.7.101	mature	4.3.35	panel	4.2.21
insight	4.3.38	maximize	1.6.82	paradigm	4.1.11
inspect	3.3.32	mechanism	4.2.18	paragraph	
instance	2.4.60	media	3.2.21	parallel	2.7.104
institute	1.5.65	mediate	4.7.93	parameter	3.1.8
instruct	2.6.86	medical	2.3.34	participate	1.1.2
integral	4.7.96	medium	4.3.35	partner	1.2.24
integrate	2.4.50	mental	2.1.11	passive	4.5.70
integrity	4.2.21	method	1.1.8	perceive	1.6.76
intelligence	2.5.69	migrate	3.1.11	percent	1.2.24
intense	3.7.97	military	4.5.60	period	1.5.71
interact	1.3.38	minimal	4.6.81	persist	4.6.76
intermediate		minimize	3.2.21	perspective	2.6.86

Word	v.u.pg	Word	v.u.pg	Word	v.u.pg
phase	2.2.28	recover	3.1.10	simulate	3.4.55
phenomenon	3.4.55	refine	4.5.67	site	1.7.90
philosophy	1.7.96	regime	4.2.27	so-called	4.5.67
physical	1.1.5	region	1.3.41	sole	3.2.18
plus	4.2.24	register	1.7.96	somewhat	3.4.52
policy	1.3.41	regulate	1.5.65	source	2.1.2
portion	4.3.35	reinforce	3.7.101	specific	1.4.53
pose	4.5.67	reject	2.3.34	specify	4.6.84
positive	1.3.32	relax	4.1.5	sphere	4.2.24
potential	1.6.76	release	3.5.60	stable	2.5.66
practitioner	4.7.99	relevant	1.6.82	statistic	2.5.72
precede	3.3.40	reluctance	4.3.38	status	2.6.80
precise	2.6.80	rely	1.4.50	straightforward	4.6.84
predict	2.1.5	remove	1.4.56	strategy	1.5.62
predominant	3.7.90	require	1.2.27	stress	2.1.2
preliminary	4.4.51	research	1.4.53	structure	1.4.56
presume	3.4.49	reside	1.5.65	style	2.3.37
previous	1.4.46	resolve	2.4.50	submit	3.6.81
primary	1.5.71	resource	1.4.53	subordinate	4.5.60
prime	2.6.80	restrain	4.6.84	subsequent	2.7.100
principal	2.7.94	restrict	1.7.93	subsidy	3.5.66
principle	1.4.56	retain	2.7.97	substitute	2.6.89
prior	3.3.37	reveal	3.1.5	successor	3.3.40
proceed	4.6.84	revenue	2.6.89	sufficient	2.4.57
process	1.2.24	reverse	3.5.63	sum	2.3.40
professional	2.1.2	revise	3.6.81	summary	2.7.104
prohibit	3.5.63	revolution	4.4.48	supplement	4.4.54
project	2.3.34	revise	3.6.81	survey	1.3.35
promote	2.7.97	role	1.6.76	survive	3.5.69
proportion	2.4.53	route	4.7.99	suspend	4.7.93
prospect	3.6.84	scenario	4.7.96	sustain	2.3.34
protocol	4.7.99	schedule	3.2.27	symbol	2.4.60
psychology		scheme	2.7.100	tape	4.1.5
publication	3.5.66	scope	3.6.81	target	2.1.11
publish	2.2.18	section	1.2.27	task	1.2.27
purchase	1.5.62	sector	1.6.85	team	4.2.24
pursue	2.5.69	secure	1.3.38	technical	4.1.8
qualitative	4.6.81	seek	1.6.82	technique	1.7.90
quote	3.3.37	select	1.3.35	technology	1.3.38
radical	3.7.90	sequence	1.7.100	temporary	4.3.38
random	3.2.27	sex		tense	3.4.46
range	1.6.79	series	2.1.8	terminate	3.6.84
ratio	3.1.8	shift	2.7.100	text	1.3.35
rational	3.4.49	significance	1.3.41	theme	3.7.94
react	1.6.85	similar	1.1.11	theory	1.6.79

Word	v.u.pg
thereby	3.7.101
thesis	3.2.27
topic	3.5.69
trace	3.6.77
tradition	1.2.27
transfer	1.5.68
transform	3.4.55
transit	2.3.43
transmit	3.5.63
transport	3.1.11
trend	2.6.83
trigger	4.7.93
ultimate	3.5.63
undergo	4.4.48
underlie	3.1.2
undertake	2.7.94
uniform	3.7.97
unify	4.5.67
unique	3.3.40
utilize	3.1.11
valid	2.2.18
vary	1.2.27
vehicle	3.7.94
version	2.4.53
via	3.7.94
violate	4.6.84
virtual	3.7.97
visible	3.5.80
vision	4.5.67
visual	4.1.8
volume	2.7.97
voluntary	3.5.69
welfare	2.6.83
whereas	4.1.11
whereby	4.7.96
widespread	3.4.49

APPENDIX B
ROOTS, PREFIXES, SUFFIXES

COMMON ROOTS, PREFIXES AND SUFFIXES IN ACADEMIC VOCABULARY

Academic vocabulary is mainly of Latin or Greek origin, so knowing common Greek and Latin roots, prefixes, and suffixes can be very helpful in learning and remembering academic vocabulary. The following tables list some common roots and affixes along with their meanings and examples. The examples in bold are words from the Academic Word List.

LATIN ROOTS

Roots	Meaning	Examples
act	to do, drive	**interact, compact, extract**
ann, enn	year	**annual,** bicentennial
aqu	water	aquarium, aqueduct
aud	to hear	auditorium, auditor
bell	war	belligerent, bellicose
cede	to go, to yield	**precede,** concede
cent	one hundred	**percent,** centennial
cept, capt, cip, cap, ceive, ceipt	to take hold, grasp	**conceive,** receive, capture
cert	to be sure, to trust	certain, certify
cess, ced	to go, to yield	**process,** successor, cessation
cid, cis	to cut off, be brief, to kill	concise, homicide
circ, circum	around	**circumstance,** circumference
clin	to lean, lie, bend	**decline, incline**
cog	to think, consider	recognize, cognitive
cor, cord, card	heart	coronary, cardiology
corp	body	**corporate,** corpse
cred	to believe, to trust	**credit,** credible
crit, cris	to separate, judge	**criteria** , criticism
culp	fault, blame	culprit, culpable
dic, dict	to say, to speak, to assert	**contradict, predict**
duct, duc	to lead, to draw	**conduct, deduce**
dur	hard, lasting	**duration,** durable
ego	I	egotistical, egocentric
equ	equal, fair	**equation,** equator
fac, fic, fect, fact	to make, do	**facilitate, affect**
fer	to carry, bear, bring	**transfer, infer, confer**
fin	end, limit	**definite, finite, confine**
flu	to flow	**fluctuations,** fluid
form	shape	**uniform** , formula, **transform**
fort	strong	fortify, fortress
fum	smoke, scent	perfume, fumigate
gen	race, family, kind	**generation, gender**
grad, gress	step, degree, rank	**grade,** gradual
grat	pleasing, thankful	grateful, congratulate
grav, griev	heavy	gravity, grieve, grave
hab	to have, hold, to dwell	habitat, habit
hom	man, human	homicide, homage
init	to begin, enter upon	**initial, initiate**
jur, jus, judic	law, right, judgment	**justify, adjust,** judicial
juven	young	juvenile, rejuvenate
laud	praise	laud, laudable
leg	law	**legal, legislate**
liber	free	**liberal, liberate**

Roots	Meaning	Examples
loc	place	**location, allocate,** local
manu	hand	**manual,** manuscript
med, medi	middle	**medium, mediate,** mediocre
medic	physician, to heal	**medical,** medicine
memor	mindful	memorial, memorable
mon	to remind, advise, warn	**monitor, demonstrate**
ment	mind	**mental, mentality**
migr	to move, travel	**immigration, migration**
mit, mis	to send	**transmit,** submit
mort	death	mortal, mortality
mov, mob, mot	to move	**remove,** mobile, motion
mut	change, exchange	mutate, mutant
nomen, nomin	name, meaning	nominate, synonym
null, nihil, nil	nothing, void	nihilism, nullify
ped	foot	pedestrian, pedestal
pend, pond, pens	to weigh, pay, to consider	**compensate,** pension, pensive
plur, plus	more	**plus,** surplus
port	to carry	**export, transport**
pos	to place, put	**dispose, impose, expose**
pot	powerful	**potential,** potent
prim, prin	first	**primary, prime**
reg, rig, rect	to rule, right, straight	**regulation,** rigid
rupt	to break, burst	disrupt, interrupt, rupture
sacr, secr, sanct	sacred	sacrifice, sanctify
sat, satis	enough	satisfy, satiate
scrib, script	to write	inscribe, subscription
sed, sid, sess	to sit, to settle	sedate, sediment, subside
sent, sens	to feel	sentimental, sense
sequ, secut	to follow, sequence	**consequence, sequence, subsequent**
sumil, simul, sembl	like,	**similar, simulation**
sol, soli	alone, lonely	**solely, isolate**
spec, spect, spic	to see, look at, behold	**perspective, inspect**
spond, spons	to pledge, promise	**respond, correspond**
tac, tic	silent	**tacit, taciturn**
ten, tain, tent	to hold	**obtain, retain, attain**
tend, tens	to stretch, strive	**tension, tendon**
termin	boundary, limit	**terminate, terminal**
test	to witness, affirm	attest, testify
tract	to pull, draw	**contract, extract**
trib	to allot, give	**distribute, contribute**
vac	empty	evacuate, vacuous
ven, vent	to come	**convention, intervene**
ver	truth	verify, veracity
vers, vert	to turn	**convert, reverse, controversy**
via	way, road	**via,** viaduct
vir	manliness, worth	virile, virtue
vis, vid	to see, look	**visible, revision, visual**
viv, vit	life	vital, vivacious
voc, vok	voice, call	**invoke, vocal, revoke**

Roots	Meaning	Examples
GREEK ROOTS		
anthropo	human being	anthropology, philanthropic
aster, astro	star	asteroid, astronomy
bio	life	biography, biology
chrom	color	chromatic, chromosome
chrono	time	chronology, chronometer
cosmo	world, order, universe	cosmos, cosmopolitan
crac, crat	rule, govern	aristocrat, democracy
dem	people	**demonstrate,** epidemic
derm	skin	dermatology, hypodermic
ethno	nation	ethnic, ethnocentric
eu	good, well	euphoric, euphemism
gam	marriage	monogamy, polygamy
geo	earth	geology, geodynamics
gno, kno	to know	knowledge, diagnostic
graph gram	to write, draw, record	telegraph, telegram
gymno, gymn	athletic	gymnasium, gymnastics
hydro	water	hydrogen, hydroplane
hypno	sleep	hypnosis, hypnotize
hypo	under, below	**hypothesis,** hypodermic
logue, logo	idea, word, speech, reason	**logic, ideological**
meter, metr	measure	**parameters,** metric
micro	small	microscope, microorganism
mim	copy	mimic, mime
mono	one	monogram, monogamy
mor	fool	moron, moronic
morph	form, structure, shape	morphology, metamorphosis
neur, nero	nerve	neural, neurotic
opt	eye	optic, optician
ortho	straight	orthodontist, orthopedics
pan	all	**expansion,** pantheism
path	feeling, disease	sympathy, pathologist
phe	speak, spoken about	prophet, euphemistic
phil, philo	love	**philosophy,** philanthropist
phob	fear	phobia, claustrophobia
phon	sound, voice	telephone, phonograph
photo	light	photosynthesis, photography
pneu	breath	pneumonia, pneumatic
polis, polit	citizen, city, state	political, metropolitan
poly	many	polygamy, polytechnic
pseudo	false	pseudo, pseudonym
psych	mind, soul, spirit	psychic, psychology
pyr	fire	pyromania, pyrotechnic
scope	to see	**scope,** telescope
soph	wise	**philosophy,** sophisticated
sym, syn	together	**symbolic,** synthesize
techn	art, skill	**technical, technology**
tele	at a distance	telescope, telephone
the, them, thet	to place, put	**hypothesis,** epithet
thea, theatr	to see, view	theatre, theatrical
theo	God	**theory,** theology
therm	heat	thermometer, thermal

PREFIXES

Prefix	Meaning	Examples
ab-	from, away from	absent, **abnormal**
ad-	to, motion toward, addition to	**advocate, administrate, adapt**
aero-	air	aerobic, aerospace
a-, an-	without	atonal, anarchy
ante-	before	antecedent, anteroom
anti-	against, opposite, reverse	anti-aircraft, antibiotics
ap-	to, nearness to	**approximate, appoint**
auto-	self	**automatic,** autograph
bene-	good	**benefit,** benefactor
bi-	two	**biannual,** bifocal
co-, con-	together	**community, cooperative, coordination , context**
contra-	against	**contrast, controversy, contradiction**
de-	opposite of, away from, undo	**deduction, decline**
dis-	opposite	**displace, disproportion**
ex-	out, beyond, away from, former	**exclude, export, external**
extra-	outside, beyond, besides	extraordinary, extracurricular
fore-	before	foreword, forecast
hyper-	more than normal, too much	hyperactive, hypersensitive
il-	not	**illegal, illogical**
im-	into	**impact, imply, immigrate**
im-	not	**immature,** imbalance
in-	not	**incapable, indiscreet, inaccurate**
inter-	among, between	**interaction, intervention, interval**
intra-	within	intramural, intrastate
ir-	not	**irrelevant, irrational**
mal-	wrong, bad	malfunction, malpractice
mis-	wrong, bad, no, not	misinterpret, misbehave
non-	not, opposite of	nontraditional, nonconformist
per-	through	**perceive, perspective**
post-	after	postgraduate, postglacial
pre-	before	**precede, previous, preliminary**
pro-	before, for, in support of	**promote,** prologue
pro-	forward	**project, proceed**
re-	back, again	**reassess, recreate, redefine**
retro-	backward	retroactive, retrospect
self-	of the self	self-respect, self-taught
semi-	half, partly	semiformal, semi-circle
sub-	under, beneath	**subordinate,** submarine
sur-	over, above	surcharge, surpass, **survey**
trans-	across, over	**transition, transport**
ultra-	extremely	ultramodern, ultrasonic
un-	not, lack of, opposite	**uninvolved, unreliable, unaware**

SUFFIXES

Suffix	Meaning	Examples
-able, -ible	can, able to	detectable, accessible, flexible
-age	action or process	percentage, linkage, voyage
-al, -ial	of, like, relating to, suitable for	cultural, traditional, potential
-ance	act, process, quality, state of being	maintenance, reliance, assurance
-ant	one who	assistant, participant
-ary	of, like, relating to	temporary, primary, voluntary
-ate	characteristic of, to become	alternate, demonstrate, eliminate
-cle, -icle	small	particle, cubicle
-cy	fact, or state of being	policy, residency
-dom	state or quality of	random, boredom
-ence	act or state of being	evidence, sequence, intelligence
-ent	doing, having, showing	consistent, sufficient, inherent
-er	one who, that which	consumer, achiever
-ery	place for, act, practice of	recovery, robbery
-ess	female	princess, goddess
-ful	full of	stressful, insightful
-ic	relating to, characteristic of	economic, specific, academic
-ify	to make, to cause to be	identify, unify
-ion	act, condition, result of,	conclusion, evaluation
-ish	of or belonging to, characterized by	stylish, selfish
-ism	act, practice, or result of, example	individualism, professionalism
-ity	condition, state of being	security, maturity, stability
-ive	of, relating to, belonging to	negative, alternative, legislative
-ize	make, cause to be, subject to	civilize, energize, finalize
-less	without	ceaseless, jobless
-logue	speech	dialogue, monologue
-logy	study or theory of	psychology, ideology
-ly	every	annually, daily
-ly	in (a specified manner, to a specified extent)	normally, automatically
-ment	action or process	commitment, assessment, adjustment
-ment	state or quality of	refinement, amusement
-ment	product or thing	environment, document
-ness	state or quality of being	awareness, uniqueness, intenseness
-or	one who	minor, actor
-ous	having, full of, characterized by	ambiguous, enormous, erroneous
-ship	state or quality of being	partnership, authorship
-some	like, tending to be	bothersome, noisome
-tude	state of quality of being	attitude, solitude
-y	characterized by	contemporary, voluntary, contrary

Reference:
Elliot, Norbert. Vocabulary Workshop. Austin, Texas: Holt, Rinehart and Winston, 2001.

CPSIA information can be obtained
at www.ICGtesting.com
Printed in the USA
FFOW03n1753160816
26858FF